Acceptance with Joy

By

Dr. Lydia A. Woods

Channing and Watt Publishers
Atlanta, GA

Acceptance with Joy, Copyright © 2000 Lydia A. Woods

Poems by Revelation, Copyright © 1995 Lydia A. Woods

For the Edification of the Saints, Copyright © 1996 Lydia A. Woods

Food for Saints, Copyright © 1997 Lydia A. Woods

Let Those With Ears..., Copyright © 1998 Lydia A. Woods

Conversations with the Saints, Copyright © 1999 Lydia A. Woods

All rights reserved.

Channing and Watt Publishers
75 Gammon Ave SE Apt #A
Atlanta, Georgia 30315
www.channingandwatt.com

Front Cover Photo and Cover Design by
Jacqueline D. Woods/JD Woods Consulting

Back Cover Photo by
Elizabeth J. Jackson

No part of this publication may be reproduced, stored in a retrieval system, copied in any form or by any means, electronic, mechanical, photocopying, recording or otherwise transmitted without written permission from the publisher. You must not circulate this book in any format without permission in writing from the author or publisher. For permissions contact Channing and Watt Publishers at:

info@channingandwatt.com

First Edition, Copyright © 2000 Lydia A. Woods
Second Edition, Copyright © 2014 Lydia A. Woods
Third Edition, Copyright © 2014 Lydia A. Woods

Printed in the United States of America

ISBN-13: 978-1-941200-26-1
LCCN: 2001088529

Other Publications by Dr. Lydia A. Woods

Poems by Revelation
For the Edification of the Saints
Food for Saints
Let Those With Ears...
Conversations with the Saints
All the Saints Agree
Those Bible Characters
Lessons of a Handmaiden
The Movies: Their Spiritual Messages
The Joy of the Lord
Under the Rainbow

Dedicated to
My Parents with Love
Mildred and Charles Woods

Acknowledgements

A piece of creative work is usually produced in isolation, but the distribution for others to see and appreciate takes many hearts and hands and minds. I want to give thanks to my friends and family members who are those hearts which support and lift me up and forward.

Special thanks to William C. Terry, Yehonatan Meru, and Veronica Norris for taking their time to proofread this book.

My appreciation to the host of colleagues, students and fellow Christian brothers and sisters who praise and encourage me and constantly remind me of the work God can do in a willing but frightened and fragile vessel.

Thank you Holy Spirit for using my humble vessel and letting me put my name on these words.

Introduction

Under the inspiration of the Holy Spirit, I began writing Christian Poetry. The Spirit would "overshadow" me as the old folk used to say and I would copy down what was given. The Spirit would leave and return again several months later. This continued for about five years until there was enough poetry for me to begin questioning the Lord as to the purpose of this gift. He instructed me to begin to put the poems all in one place in an orderly format. The first book, entitled "Poems by Revelation," was the result. While putting the book in publishable form the Spirit became extremely active which led to a second collection of poems and thus, I began on the unlikely path of author/publisher.

These collections of poems are inspired by the lessons which the Lord has been teaching me over years of walking with Him. Many poems are inspired by uplifting and stimulating conversations with God's precious saints and others are born out of frustration from ungodliness and ignorance of God's Word which exist around me.

In reading, I hope you will find poems which speak to your heart and express what you have experienced on your walk with the Father. The writing of these poems allows me an outlet of expression as the Lord tempers and prepares me for my calling.

Table of Contents

Poems
Poems by Revelation

A Bible Character	1
Birthright	3
Bringing His Family Out	5
The Day of His Birth	7
Doin' the Israelite	9
Get a Testimony	13
Getting to Know You	15
Good News	17
Good News II	19
It's Adoption Time	21
It's War!	23
Joseph	25
Just Do It!	29
Master of Masters	31
No Abundance in the Wilderness	33
Put It All On!	35
Quest for Salvation	37
Simply Because You Are Mine	39
So Be Like Job	41
What's His Face?	43

For the Edification of the Saints

Adult vs Child 47
But For Your Praying Saints 49
Created in My Father's Image 51
Don't Envy Those 53
The Family Business 55
Fear vs Faith 57
Go the Distance 59
God Will Provide 63
Group Three 65
Hedge of Protection 67
How Many Times 69
How Will I Know Him? 72
I Need the Eyes of Jesus 73
If You Want to Make God Laugh! 75
In a Split Second 77
The Inside of the Cup 81
It's Not About Money 83
Oh! To be Like the Master 85
Somethin' Told Me 91
Take a Visit to the Upper Room 93
The Time is Short! 97
Was He Saved? Did He Know the Lord? 99

Food for Saints

- Above All 103
- Be Still! 105
- Children of the King 107
- Doin' the Adam 109
- Father Knows Best 111
- For the Elect's Sake 113
- Get in the House 117
- God's M.O. 119
- I'm Not Lucky – I'm Blessed! 121
- I'm Tired! 123
- If You Loved Me Lord… 127
- It's Alright 129
- Just Wait! 130
- Know Your Enemy 131
- Lean Not 133
- Love is an Action 134
- So What's-Up With That! 135
- Take Out the Trash! 137
- Unable to Receive 139
- With Persecution… 141

Let Those With Ears...

Answer to Many a Prayer 145
Blood Disguise 147
Boys Into Men 149
The Building You Call Church 151
Don't Forsake the Assembly 152
E.T. 153
Fruit Trees 155
Generations in You 158
The Gift 159
Has Done, Is Doing or Will Do 161
Holy Rollers 163
Jesus Learned Obedience 165
Just Give It! 169
Liar, Liar 171
My God Isn't Stupid! 175
Not in a Place Called Church 176
Obedience the Highest Form of Praise 177
The Perfect Murder 179
Resistance is Futile 181
So Great a Cloud of Witnesses 183
The U.P.S. Man 187
Upside Down, Inside Out 188
With His Own Blood 189

Conversations with the Saints

Ain't He All That! 193
A Blessing – Not a Curse! 195
Call My Name 197
Cerebral Palsy 198
Common Sense 199
Convicted 201
Denominations 203
Forgive or Forgive Not 204
He's Good At… 205
If Thou Be… 207
If You Will Be Great 209
Just a Family Feud 211
The Kingdom is Like Unto… 213
Love You - Not Your Sin 215
Only Human! 217
Pro-Choice? 219
Puzzling 221
Sabbath Day 223
Seeds of Self-Destruction 225
Take No Thought 227
There But For the Grace… 228
Tower of Babel 229
True Way of Life 231
What's Your Problem? 233

Scriptural References
Poems by Revelation

A Bible Character	237
Birthright	240
Bringing His Family Out	247
The Day of His Birth	249
Doin' the Israelite	250
Get a Testimony	252
Getting to Know You	253
Good News	254
Good News II	256
It's Adoption Time	262
It's War!	263
Joseph	264
Just Do It!	267
Master of Masters	268
No Abundance in the Wilderness	271
Put It All On!	272
Quest for Salvation	273
Simply Because You Are Mine	274
So Be Like Job	275
What's His Face?	276

For the Edification of the Saints

Adult vs Child 278
But For Your Praying Saints 279
Created in My Father's Image 280
Don't Envy Those 281
The Family Business 282
Fear vs Faith 283
Go the Distance 284
God Will Provide 290
Group Three 292
Hedge of Protection 294
How Many Times 296
How Will I Know Him? 297
I Need the Eyes of Jesus 304
If You Want to Make God Laugh! 305
In a Split Second 306
The Inside of the Cup 307
It's Not About Money 308
Oh! To be Like the Master 310
Somethin' Told Me 311
Take a Visit to the Upper Room 312
The Time is Short! 314
Was He Saved? Did He Know the Lord? 317

Food for Saints

- Above All 319
- Be Still! 320
- Children of the King 321
- Doin' the Adam 322
- Father Knows Best 325
- For the Elect's Sake 326
- Get in the House 327
- God's M.O. 328
- I'm Not Lucky – I'm Blessed! 329
- I'm Tired! 331
- If You Loved Me Lord… 332
- It's Alright 333
- Just Wait! 334
- Know Your Enemy 335
- Lean Not 337
- Love is an Action 338
- So What's-Up With That! 339
- Take Out the Trash! 340
- Unable to Receive 341
- With Persecution… 342

Let Those With Ears...

Answer to Many a Prayer 345
Blood Disguise 346
Boys Into Men 347
The Building You Call Church 348
Don't Forsake the Assembly 349
E.T. 350
Fruit Trees 351
Generations in You 352
The Gift 353
Has Done, Is Doing or Will Do 354
Holy Rollers 355
Jesus Learned Obedience 356
Just Give It! 357
Liar, Liar 358
My God Isn't Stupid! 359
Not in a Place Called Church 360
Obedience the Highest Form of Praise 361
The Perfect Murder 362
Resistance is Futile 363
So Great a Cloud of Witnesses 365
The U.P.S. Man 366
Upside Down, Inside Out 367
With His Own Blood 369

Conversations with the Saints

Ain't He All That! 371
A Blessing – Not a Curse! 372
Call My Name 373
Cerebral Palsy 374
Common Sense 375
Convicted 376
Denominations 377
Forgive or Forgive Not 379
He's Good At… 380
If Thou Be... 382
If You Will Be Great 383
Just a Family Feud 384
The Kingdom is Like Unto… 385
Love You - Not Your Sin 390
Only Human! 391
Pro-Choice? 392
Puzzling 393
Sabbath Day 394
Seeds of Self-Destruction 395
Take No Thought 396
There But For the Grace... 397
Tower of Babel 399
True Way of Life 400
What's Your Problem? 401

Scriptural Index 402

Alphabetical Listing of Poems 412

Poems

Poems by Revelation

Dr. Lydia A. Woods

A Bible Character

Luke 22:47, 57, 60; 23:21-34; Mark 15:1, 10-11, 16:1;
Matthew 21:24; I Peter 2:9 (KJV)

I've heard the Holy Book called the, "Living Word,"
It lives and breathes, and strains to be heard.
And I heard a Saint say, I'd like to be,
A Bible character for all to see.

No sooner said, than the chance came their way,
The Word leapt from the page to the everyday.
And all of a sudden that Word came alive,
The Holy Spirit had heard and opportunity arrived.

It's an honor to be on the battlefield,
In the perilous days when warfare is real.
We'll all get our chance to stand for Christ,
And prove to everyone that we're bought with a price.

Which character will you be on that Bible stage,
If the casting is done and war is waged?
Are you Judas, who comes with kisses by night,
Or Pilate who washes the blood out of sight?

Are you in the crowd crying crucify Him,
Or Peter who denies that he is His friend?
Or the soldiers who cast lots for His garment in greed
Or the wicked leaders who arranged the deed?

Are you one of the twelve who walked with Him,
But couldn't be found when the evening grew dim?
Were you one of the women, He delivered from sin,
But remembered that He said, "He would rise again?"

Acceptance with Joy

Even though they were afraid, they went to the tomb,
To give honor to their Lord and His body groom.
Will you be counted with the very few,
Who waited on the Lord as their hope grew?

And believed all He'd said would come true,
That He would return for me and you
And in the meantime, while we're on earth,
Washed in His blood, a child of new birth.

Just check yourself out in every way,
And see which role you'll play today.
Could they cast you for peculiar people indeed,
The Royal Priesthood and Child of His seed?

Called by His name and set aside,
The Temple of God, let His Spirit abide.
In the beauty of Holiness tried and true,
Let His Spirit be found in me and you.

Dr. Lydia A. Woods

Birthright

Genesis 27:1-46; 28:1-22 (KJV)

The story of Jacob and Esau is over the top,
I started reading about them and could not stop.
You should check it out when I am through,
'Cause it will speak, I'm sure, directly to you!

I bet you didn't know that they were twins,
Jacob was second to come out, so Esau did win.
The right to inherit all his father's wealth and land,
Jacob was on the out – but his mother had a plan.

Jacob was her favorite son you see,
She wanted Jacob to inherit, but this is the key.
Isaac's blessing would go only to the one,
Who would inherit – Esau the favorite son.

So she plotted to get that blessing you know,
And Jacob helped in the deception just so.
He got his brother to sell his birthright for food,
Now taking his brother's birthright was a bit rude.

They were very different these twins indeed,
One was smooth the other hairy – now take heed.
How could Jacob fool this blind old man,
He would know when he touched Jacob's hand.

So he covered his hands and neck with fur skins,
It did the trick and the blessing Jacob did win.
His brother's blessing he took in a flash,
Forever his – and that blessing would last.

Acceptance with Joy

Esau hated his brother for what he had done,
He swore to kill him – put Jacob on the run.
Now you know what goes around comes again,
Jacob's treachery would visit him in the end.

And so it did in a far off land,
He fell in love with the daughter of his Uncle Laban.
He worked seven years to win her hand,
But on the wedding night Laban had a plan.

He tricked Jacob and put Leah in his bed,
And bargained seven more years before he could wed,
His beloved Rachel – so the trick was done,
But more grief to Jacob was waiting to come.

Rachel couldn't have that precious child,
Trouble was stirring in this marriage all the while.
Jacob had ten sons before his favorite came,
Rachel finally had a son and Joseph was his name.

So remember when you set out to do no good,
It just comes rolling back seven-fold as it should.
God will give you all your blessings indeed,
Don't take someone else's in your greed.

Dr. Lydia A. Woods

Bringing His Family Out

Genesis 3:22-24; Mark 1:14-15; I Peter 2:9; I Corinthians 2:12; Ephesians 1:3-6; Acts 2:17; Matthew 24:21-22; Hebrews 10:38 (KJV)

My beloved, There's a secret I'll reveal to you,
Of God's glorious plan tried and true.
You remember of old, how Adam fell,
And condemned us all to eternal hell?

God turned His face from man that day,
The sin we bore made Him put us away.
Satan didn't know God was a step ahead,
And had a plan for him and his final bed.

God's precious Son said, that He would go,
Into the world and let the people know,
Of the Father's love, and of His life giving Word.
Of which the world had never really heard.

Of His glorious Kingdom Jesus testified,
And the people knew that the Pharisee's had lied.
God wanted a people to call His own,
Who would follow His Word, into the unknown.

And walk by faith - blind - without natural sight,
But would trust in Him with all their might.
A peculiar people to the world they would be,
But this sets us apart both you and me.

A Compilation of Christian Poetry   *Poems by Revelation*

Acceptance with Joy

We're a race of beings that has never been before,
Born of the Spirit that come to God by just one door.
Through the blood of His Son, His family shines pure,
The Righteousness of God of that I am sure.

We are scattered in the world called by name,
Joined by One Spirit which makes us the same.
Brothers and sisters laborers in the field,
Working to increase God's family yield.

His Holy Spirit is the key to unlocking the truth,
With revelation knowledge you'll have the proof,
That we are living in perilous times, these last days,
So live by faith and truth in all your ways.

It won't be long, then we'll be homeward bound,
The signs of this are all around.
God's plan is being fulfilled as I speak,
Keep the faith, be strong, steadfast not weak.

God has shortened the time for the Elects' sake,
Jesus is coming soon with Saints in His wake.
God's glorious plan is working like a charm,
He's bringing His family out by His mighty arm.

Dr. Lydia A. Woods

The Day of His Birth

Genesis 1:26-27; Luke 2:6-14 (KJV)

The Lord created man from the dust of the earth,
He breathed life into him and gave him birth.

He gave him dominion and power beyond compare,
But man betrayed His trust, on Satan's dare.

But the Lord was ready with plans of His own,
To bring His Son to earth from His golden throne.

He was born in a manger on Christmas day,
There was no room in the inn so the scriptures say.

Three came to worship Him from near and far,
They were guided by the light of the brightest star.

Three wise men brought Him incense, myrrh, and gold,
The shepherds left their flocks as they were told.

The Heavenly Host did sing of His new Birth,
Of Good Will Toward Men and Peace on Earth.

Dr. Lydia A. Woods

Doin' the Israelite

Exodus 11:2, 13:21, 14:27-28, 16:2-3,12, 17:2-4 (KJV)

Have you ever thought after reading about,
How the Lord brought the Israelites out?
Just how they could murmur and complain,
It boggles my mind and spins my brain.

I call it, "Doin' the Israelite!"

I couldn't imagine after all God had done,
Wanting to turn back high-tail-it and run.
Back to bondage and the Pharaoh's whip,
And not wanting to make that glorious trip.

I call it, "Doin' the Israelite!"

After bringing them out with silver and gold,
Every man, woman, child from the young to the old.
After parting the sea and walking on dry land,
And destroying the enemy with a sweep of his hand.

I call it, "Doin' the Israelite!"

How could they slip back to their ungodly way,
While Moses was getting what God had to say
On the tablets of stone Gods' glorious Word,
Of which His people had never heard.

I call it, "Doin' the Israelite!"

Now remember how He led them by night and by day,
Leading them so evident all of the way.
And all of the miracles and the wondrous feats,
Water from stone and manna to eat.

I call it, "Doin' the Israelite!"

Acceptance with Joy

He kept them better than the birds or the lilies of the field,
It's hard to comprehend, it can't really be real,
But now as I take my wilderness walk,
Sometimes I have to check my thoughts and my talk.

Am I, "Doin' the Israelite?"

I find that, I too, murmur and complain,
And sometimes I think I'll go insane.
I know the Spirit of God dwells in me,
And I should walk by faith unable to see.

Am I, "Doin' the Israelite?"

It isn't as easy, as it looks,
I thought it would be, after reading His book.
His account of the Israelites warns all of us,
Of the possible fate if we doubt and mistrust.

Are you, "Doin' the Israelite?"

Saints, believe what I'm about to say,
You will do the Israelite every day.
Yes, I'm telling it right and telling it straight,
We are all filled, with fear, mistrust and hate.

Are you, "Doin' the Israelite?"

Lord, help and forgive me, I repent and ask,
For strength and understanding, so I can last.
The entire way to the Promise land,
Don't leave me in the wilderness, bring me out by your hand.

Poems by Revelation   *A Compilation of Christian Poetry*

Dr. Lydia A. Woods

I don't want to be caught, "Doin' the Israelite!"

Lord I want to be found steadfast and true,
Faithful to the end, believing in You.
You never said, it would be easy or a piece of cake,
But that tribulation would come, and it's for our sakes.

I'm growing in faith every day,
I believe you'll perfect me in every way.
But it's not because I am so good,
Or because I have faith like I should.

But because You are faithful and true to Your Word,
And what You have started, You'll finish, I've heard.
And in the end, everything will be right,
And I won't be caught, "Doin' the Israelite!"

Dr. Lydia A. Woods

Get a Testimony

Luke 4:18-19; James 1:2-4 (KJV)

The Lord showed me a truth some time ago,
When I was just reborn about a month or so.

To testify of the Father Jesus came,
To make known His Kingdom and to proclaim,
Of what He knew to be the truth of His Father's love.
And to send the Holy Spirit to us like a dove.

Well, it dawned on me what was going on,
Our walk with God is no different from His Son's!
Our mission like His is the same for me and you,
We need to proclaim what we know of the Father too.

How can we do that if not for tribulation and trial,
So a personal witness we become, our testimony to compile.
For the testimony as the Lord explained it to me.
Is Anointed from above, speak it out and see.

Now there are certain ones that the Lord will send on your path.
It's time to tell your testimony that's really your task.
It's not for everyone you meet,
But to those whom the Father sends - it is so sweet.

They will be edified and surely lifted up.
As the anointing flows and they drink from that cup.
You know for a fact of what He's done for you.
How you overcame and He saw you through.

A Compilation of Christian Poetry *Poems by Revelation*

Acceptance with Joy

Once you are born again, and tribulation comes,
You begin to make that testimony one by one.
You have so many miracles of what He's done for you,
You can't even count them if you tried to.

When I think about all He's done on my walk,
I get real happy and just talk and talk.
I experience a feeling of elevation,
My spirit soars with pure elation.

Sometimes I testify well into the night,
My spirit is renewed and filled with delight.
I am floating three feet above the floor.
I just want to talk about Him more and more.

This feeling lasts long after I am through,
Are you listening well 'cause I'm talking to you.
So get yourself a testimony of the Father's Love.
Get on the job, your orders are straight from above.

Get yourself a testimony, not someone else's, you see,
Yours is Anointed for you, and you're in good company.
For Jesus testified of the Father and what He knew,
We each have our own and there's one waiting for you!

Dr. Lydia A. Woods

Getting to Know You

Proverbs 1:7, 2:1, 3:1-4 (KJV)

Lord, it's been a joy just getting to know You,
Through the hard times, when You carried me through.
Our friendship has grown and blossomed over the years.
Through it all You've eased my mind and calmed my fears.

Your nature is sweet and loving and kind,
Your patience with me, sometimes blows my mind.
We have a special relationship, You and me,
It's something that no one else can see.

Your Spirit speaks to mine throughout the day,
I'm not always listening to what You have to say.
I get caught up in the cares of this crazy world,
And sometimes my flesh keeps my mind in a whirl.

Then You remind me of what Your Word said,
About renewing my mind, not relying on my own head.
Walking by the Spirit and not by sight,
Living every day without fear or fright,

Of what tomorrow will bring or what the bill collectors' say,
But letting You guide my footsteps day by day.
I'm better today than yesterday and further along this path,
I'm holding on to faith and enduring to the last.

Where I am weak You are very strong,
Through You, I can do all things, I can't go wrong.
I'm practicing resting in You with every trial,
I know Your work in me will take a while.

Acceptance with Joy

I can see the changes as I look back,
That's what keeps me going, steady on this track.
I have tasted of Your goodness, it's fine and sweet.
I'm looking forward to when face to face we meet.

I hope it won't be long, please don't tarry Dear,
I'll be ready and waiting, for the Bridegroom here.
In a place that is not my real true home,
Take me back to the life where I belong.

Where peace and joy are ever present there,
Where angels sing Your praises and everyone will share.
In glorifying the Father and Son both day and night,
And Love will abound and all things will finally be right.

Dr. Lydia A. Woods

Good News

I Corinthians 15:3, 15:52; Mark 13:24-27; Revelation 1:7, 19:7-9, 20:1-3, 21:1-5 (KJV)

Jesus died on the cross, for our souls,
He took our sickness in His body, so it was told.

That's how it all began a long time ago,
I'm not telling no tales that you don't know.

Brothers and sisters you better listen up,
And take a long cool drink from the Jesus cup.

It's time we all got saved, in these terrible times,
You know the rapture's comin', don't be left behind.

He's comin' in the clouds, in a twinkle of an eye,
You know the Saints that are living, will not die.

So believe in Him and in the power of His might,
'Cause He's coming like a thief, in the night.

And then there's seven long years, of hell on earth,
It's the tribulation times, Thank God for His Birth!

'Cause the Saints will be rockin' at the marriage feast,
And those here on earth will be fighting the beast.

Now He's coming back to set up His reign,
The earth will be changed, it won't be the same.

Acceptance with Joy

We're all coming back as Kings and Priest,
We won't have to contend with the beast.

He'll be sitting in the pit, with all of his gang,
Until Jesus is finished with His thousand year reign.

Then Satan watch out cause yo' end is near,
The lake of fire is what you fear.

Now I'm telling the truth of what the scriptures say,
There's a Holy New Jerusalem on its way.

God will dwell with men on this new earth,
No sorrow will exist in this new birth.

So get your heart right and set your mind,
And get Salvation now and put your sins behind.

I'm spreading the Good News throughout the Land,
That Jesus Christ, He is our man!
That Jesus Christ, He is our man!
That Jesus Christ, He is our man!

Dr. Lydia A. Woods

Good News II

Mark 16:15-18; Revelation 2:1-29, 3:1-22 (KJV)

I've got more Good News, in Good News II,
For years you sat in church, on that cold, hard pew.
The preacher ranted and raved about repenting from sin,
But never told of the Glory you would win.

I'm here to "Shout the Good News" at the top of my lungs,
And tell about all the good things you have won.

When Jesus did His thing on the cross that day,
He took the sins of the world forever away.
He took your sickness in His body, so get off your bed,
Get it down, in your spirit, just what I said.

God could turn His face to man again,
The Blood of His Son washed away all sin.
He could hear the cries of a world He created,
And begin His family for so long He had waited.

To institute an adoption plan,
And pass His Holy Spirit to His recreated Man.

Now Jesus rose from the dead to sit at the right hand,
A Priest that intercedes between God and Man.
Jesus had to die, to give a new testament,
And rise again, an inheritance to present.

Acceptance with Joy

So use the name of Jesus to cast the devil out,
Lay your hands on the sick and never doubt.
Eat any deadly thing it won't hurt you,
Raise the dead to life, as you were told to do.

Cause when He poured His Spirit out on you,
You became a new creature, with work to do!!
Into all the world to tell of His glory,
But that's not the end of this precious story.

BELOVED!!

I'm telling the truth of what the scriptures say,
There's a Holy New Jerusalem on its way.
God will dwell with men on this new earth,
No sorrow will exist in this new birth.

So get your heart right, and set your mind,
Get Salvation now and put your sins behind.
I'm spreading the Good News, throughout the Land,
That Jesus Christ is still our Man!
That Jesus Christ is still our Man!
That Jesus Christ is still our Man!

Dr. Lydia A. Woods

It's Adoption Time

Galatians 4:5-7; Ephesians 1:4-5 (KJV)

Man's law states that you may not abuse,
The little children, and if you're accused,
And found to misuse your parental authority,
A new Family will be found for the children, you see.

That was God's plan first, not man's you know,
For we were kidnapped from God, so long ago.
The evil deed took place in the garden that day,
And we grew-up believing what the devil had to say.

We thought he was our father, you see,
But the kidnapper had no love for you or me,
He only came to kill, and steal and destroy,
To take away our birthright and steal our joy.

But just like, in the world, in the orphanage,
A plan is set up for the unfortunate,
That's God's plan for us, from heaven above.
To take those children who have never known love.

Each orphan is waiting to be called by name,
To a family belong and be rid of the shame.
To be rescued from the pain and the grief,
Resting in their Father's arms, in grace and peace.

Acceptance with Joy

Wait no more the paperwork is done,
When Jesus died on the cross the victory was won.
For His brothers and sisters a way was made,
All who live by His Word, will surely be saved.

It's adoption time, no more abuse to bear,
It won't be long that the prince of the air,
Will get his just desserts, for his child abuse,
Just read the Holy Word don't be obtuse.

Little Children, come into His family and accept His love,
It's freely given to you from God above.

From death to life, you'll be born again,
Washed in His Blood, a stranger to sin.
You'll grow in grace every day in every way,
Surely goodness and mercy will follow you that day.

When you take Christ to be your Lord and King,
He'll make your song sweet and you will sing,
Of His grace and glory and mercy and truth,
I'm an Adoptive child of God, I am living proof.

Dr. Lydia A. Woods

It's War!

Ephesians 6:10-17 (KJV)

It's War!
When you take Jesus and you're reborn,
There's something you should know that's going on.

It's War!
In high places that you can't see,
Put on your Spiritual ears, and listen to me.

It's War!
Yeah, it's war, that I'm talking about,
When I am finished there will be no doubt.

It's War!
Against darkness and wickedness on high,
If you listen real well there's no fear you'll die!

It's War!
But the victory's yours, without a doubt,
Your Savior fought the fight and worked it all out.

It's War!
But there is a special way you fight,
You just stand still with all of your might.

It's War!
And there's a special armor you wear,
The helmet of Salvation won't muss your hair.

Acceptance with Joy

And on your loins the Truth you'll wear,
The Breastplate of Righteousness won't even tear.

You have the Gospel of Peace upon your feet,
And with the Shield in hand you won't feel the heat,

From the wicked fiery darts being thrown at you,
You don't have to despair, you know what to do.

With the Sword in hand just lift it high,
And quench those darts and watch them fly.

But you're not hurt, you only have to stand,
And be very patient and wait on your Man.

Cause He's coming in a cloud to rescue you,
The Holy One of God, Tried and True.

It's War!
And you're commanded to watch and pray,
I can hear the Lord say on that final day,

Well done good soldier - come on in,
Did you have a doubt that we would win?

And in the end, you'll be proud to say,
I had my armor on and withstood the evil day.

Poems by Revelation *A Compilation of Christian Poetry*

Dr. Lydia A. Woods

Joseph

Genesis 37:2-5, 9, 15, 31-35, 41:41-43, 45:1-5 (KJV)

In the Bible there are people whose stories are told,
I know you think they're out dated and very old.
But there's a lesson to learn for us today,
Let me lay it out in a simple way.

Now take Joseph for instance and what happened to him,
All those brothers who threw him over the rim
Of that deep dark pit, then plotted his demise,
Joseph hadn't acted cool or very wise.

Jacob loved Joseph more than the others,
This caused a lot of hate in Joseph's brothers.
And beside all that, he made Joseph that coat,
It really made the brothers mad and got their goat.

But that's not all, there's a little more,
Joseph had those dreams, so the brothers evened the score.
Into slavery they sold Joseph on that day,
Dipped the coat in blood and to Jacob did say,

That a wild beast had torn him from limb to limb,
Jacob mourned and grieved for his future was dim,
Cause his precious son was gone never to return,
He rent his clothes - his kin were very concerned.

They could not comfort him, all the daughters and sons,
And that's how Joseph's long journey had begun.

Acceptance with Joy

Joseph went through trials and tribulations galore,
He was lied on, thrown in prison, I know his heart was sore.
He missed his father and even those brothers, you see,
He had years to work out resentment, to set his soul free.

All through the bad times he held onto his God,
His masters thought him strange and very odd.
But God watched over Joseph for He had a plan,
To bring all Jacob's children to Goshen land.

Well, the day finally came and face to face they came,
Joseph and his brothers - my how Joseph had changed.
Pharaoh had set Joseph over his house and lands,
To keep them all from starving, just a part of God's plan.

Not only had Joseph changed, but the brothers too,
Joseph tested them, he gave them back their due.
They repented for the evil deed done so long ago,
But God turned it to their good, don't you know.

For that's the secret I'm about to reveal to you,
There is one in each family that God works through.
For the Salvation of the others it's a glorious plan,
Are you the one that God has cut out with His hand?

Are you the odd one, that never seems to fit in?
Praying for Salvation of all your family in the end,
Calling on the name of the Lord every day,
On your wilderness walk not seeing your way?

Dr. Lydia A. Woods

Well take heart 'cause it's all promised to you,
God will honor His Word and see your family through.
Like Joseph He'll set you on high with His Son,
He'll raise you up after you have done

Your appointed time in the wilderness,
As you cling to your God and sin resist.
See those stories aren't so old for us today,
Take heart and let them encourage you on your way!

Dr. Lydia A. Woods

Just Do It!

Mark 16:15-20 (KJV)

These signs shall follow them that believe,
Come on Saints, I know that you can read.
I found these signs in Mark sixteen and seventeen,
I didn't read about this in any comic magazine!

It says, to use His name to cast the devil out,
Don't you think that's what Saints should be about?
Jesus cast the devil out while He walked among us,
We should use His name, not fear spirits, and trust

That His Word is true, and there is power in His name.
Keep working that Word you won't be the same.
Now at first it might not look like you're doing a thing.
But in the spirit world you've created a scene.

You have rocked the house of where Satan lives.
Keep using the name until Satan gives.
Just keep it up and don't think to quit,
Cause you're commanded to ...

"Just Do It!"

It also says, with new tongues they will speak,
So get your new tongue, get power, don't be weak.
Tongues edify you not anyone else, you see,
It's evidence of the Holy Spirit in thee.

It's a gift you ask for so make that choice,
Open up your mouth and give the Holy Spirit a voice.
Praying in the Spirit is a more perfect way,
To fulfill what He's commanded us to do every day.

Acceptance with Joy

It also builds that faith and this pleases God,
I know it sounds kind of funny and you look odd.
But remember you're a peculiar people indeed.
Born of His Spirit a child of His seed.

Don't be concerned about how you look,
Cause it's written in His Holy Book.
Just keep it up and don't think to quit,
Cause you're commanded to ...

"Just Do It!"

It also says, to heal the sick,
Lay hands on them the healing is quick.
How many Saints have you seen doing this?
It doesn't take special gifts there is no risk.

They will talk about you, and probably laugh out loud,
While you are imitating the Son all the while.
Can you stand to look strange and face the doubt?
But remember that's what peculiar people are all about.

Now at first it might not look like you're doing a thing,
But in the spirit world you've created a scene.
You remind the devil that he can't stay,
He has to honor the Word and be on his way.

You have rocked the house of where Satan lives,
Keep using the name until Satan gives.
Just keep it up and don't think to quit,
Cause' you're commanded to …

"Just Do it!"

-30-

Dr. Lydia A. Woods

Master of Masters

Matthew 4:1, 4:19, 5:1, 7:29, 8:26, 11:5; Luke 8:43-48;
John 2:1-11, 11:43-44 (KJV)

The Master of Masters was a fisher of men,
He taught the people and forgave all their sin.
He was tempted of Satan in the wilderness,
But full of the Spirit He did resist.

He was pressed by the multitude from all around,
On the mountain He taught, and made the Word profound.
He delivered the sick from all their pain,
He broke down the law and made it plain.

He made the blind to see and He calmed the rain,
And healed the minds of those insane.
He turned the water to wine, at the wedding feast,
He sent foul, filthy spirits into the beast.

A woman with faith who believed in Him,
And did not believe her chances were dim.
Touched the hem of His garment and she got blessed,
And captured the virtue He did possess.

Acceptance with Joy

Now it's written all there in His Holy Book,
Just open it up and have a look.
He raised the dead to life, and made the lame to walk,
He spent time with His disciples and they did talk

About eternal life and the Father above,
And of that greatest commandment - How to Love.
He spoke in parables, so only they would know,
The ones with ears, could learn and grow,

Who open their hearts, and the Son accept,
And repent of their sins, which gives Him respect.
Cause He's the Master of Masters, the Holy One,
The Alpha and Omega, God's Beloved Son.

Dr. Lydia A. Woods

No Abundance in the Wilderness

Matthew 4:1-11 (KJV)

Take heed Saints, I'll not have you ignorant,
Some of us are in the midst of the wilderness,
We shouldn't expect every comfort or plenty,
For in the wilderness there isn't any.

In the wilderness all that can be found,
Is the Grace of the Savior we adore.
Teaching each of His precious children,
To depend on Him more and more.

In the wilderness we must become as little children,
Dependent on Him for every need.
Learning to live in a world,
Filled with jealousy, hatred, and greed.

In the wilderness you won't be quite alone,
Other children of God are also there too.
When we meet we encourage each other,
Lifting spirits and our strength renew.

The Lord commanded the Israelites gather the manna,
So they gathered according to each need,
God spoiled it when they tried to store up,
And gathered too much in their greed.

God wanted the Israelites to depend on Him,
Every day and in all of their ways,
Becoming a peculiar people not like any other race.
Looking to him, and seeking only His Face.

Acceptance with Joy

Don't try to store up treasures and material things,
Putting aside for that rainy day,
Naming it and claiming it with money to spare.
For we must completely place ourselves in His care.

For God wants to prove to us His love,
The wilderness experience is the perfect place.
Ever mindful that without Him we're not complete,
Teaching us to be humble, and without self-deceit.

For when Jesus left the wilderness after 40 days,
His ministry spread throughout the land,
He began to preach the gospel of the Kingdom,
He died and rose again for the Salvation of Man.

So when your wilderness experience is complete,
How strong and steadfast your faith will be,
You'll be rooted and grounded in the Lord,
Prepared for your ministry, not bound, completely free.

So the wilderness is just for a season,
Our needs will be met and we'll surely be blessed,
A training period to develop faith in the Lord,
But remember, "There's No Abundance in the Wilderness."

Dr. Lydia A. Woods

Put It All On!

Ephesians 6:11-17 (KJV)

God said, to put the whole armor on,
It's the gift you get when you're reborn.

Now you probably heard it many times before,
To put it on - don't let Satan in the door.

It's not too big, it fits just right,
Cause you can't fight in your own might.

The Lord wants you to be able to stand,
In the evil day and take command,

Over Satan's wickedness - put him under your feet,
It'll give you pleasure, the victory is sweet.

Have you ever thought, what would happen to you,
If you didn't obey, what God told you to do?

That's why many Saints today are laying down,
And pieces of the armor are scattered around.

'Cause they just don't know how to keep it on,
Even though they've been saved and are reborn.

Acceptance with Joy

Unless it's all on, you won't have success,
You get attacked and your life's a mess.

Those wicked fiery darts keep coming fast,
At times you feel that you won't last.

Just check yourself out, a piece is slipping down,
And before you know it, Satan's got you bound.

So keep the helmet on, your mind to protect,
Darts are aimed there, so you'll lose respect,

For the Word of God and His integrity,
Satan wants to take your joy, so your peace will flee.

And when peace is gone it's confusion there,
Some armor is missing, and you're in despair.

So renew your mind everyday -
Wash it with the Word, so you can say,

"It is written Satan -- Get behind me,"
Experience the Power of the Word and watch him flee!

Dr. Lydia A. Woods

Quest for Salvation

Malachi 3:13-18 (KJV)

We've been round and round with this old thing,
Look at the sorrow that the Quest for Salvation brings.
Every quest has its ups and downs,
Even the road to Salvation where I am bound.

It gets tough and the going is not great,
This path dips and turns, it's not very straight.
Sometimes I wonder where it all will lead,
It's not a lot of fun, being born of His Seed.

The others seem to be having lots of fun,
With their new cars and condos in the sun.
Money in the bank and plans galore,
They don't even consider God's Son – The Door,

To everlasting life and peace,
When will this perfection process cease?
I keep Your ordinances from day to day,
And others don't give a care about what You say.

Acceptance with Joy

At times I'm confused and sometimes lost,
I just want so much to please my Boss.
At times I think I'm almost there,
And soon I'll be without a care.

And then the Holy Spirit will show to me,
My inner self - I don't want to see.
That horrible person, so full of pride,
So hateful and selfish, I just can't deny.

That I'm not perfect, not ready yet,
I'm still in the making of that you can bet.
I know that one day when it's all done,
He'll look in His book and I would have won,

By no great works or goodness of my own,
He has perfected me now I'm full grown.
Into His presence now I may stand,
A Recreated Spirit and Brand New Human!

Dr. Lydia A. Woods

Simply Because You Are Mine

Matthew 7:11; I Corinthians 2:9-11; Isaiah 64:4;
Psalm 31:19 (KJV)

Have you ever been blessed by the Lord?

I have, so many times I can't even count.
And it was one day recently that I found out,
A mystery that was hidden from me,
I was blinded and I didn't really see.

A truth that I had heard many times and should know,
That Jesus loves me, for the Bible tells me so,
But we only really know in part,
And can't truly understand until He expands our heart.

And it was on that day the Lord blessed me well,
My heart was full, and the tears began to swell.
He blessed me with the secrets of my Heart,
Only He and I knew about this part.

You see, I didn't have a revelation of the depth of His love,
And revelation knowledge comes from His Spirit above.

So one day the Lord spoke softly to me,

A Compilation of Christian Poetry　　　　　*Poems by Revelation*

Acceptance with Joy

"I don't bless you because you are so good,
Or because you always behave as you should,
I bless you because I am true and just and kind,
I bless you simply because you are Mine."

He said,
"Think of how you bless your children at Christmas time,
You plan for weeks for the day when you can make their faces shine.
How much more do I too plan for mine
Hoping to see their faces shine?

Do you think that I am one who does not feel?
Sometimes I think you don't believe, I am real.
I've been working to prove to you every day,
By providing your needs and wants in every way.

That I love you, not because you are so good,
Or because you always behave as you should,
But because I am true and just and kind,
And Simply Because You Are Mine."

So Be Like Job

Job 2:13 (KJV)

Job was a mighty man of God they say,
He made offerings to God, every day.

He was perfect, upright and very devout,
And God told Satan, to check him out.

His animals and beasts were all carried away,
His servants were killed that terrible day.

A house it fell on his daughters and sons,
Only one was left, to tell all that was done.

Job ripped his clothes and was highly upset,
But he worshipped God, of that you can bet.

He blessed the name of the Lord and did not sin,
It sent Satan running back to the Lord again.

Acceptance with Joy

This time Satan set out to do bodily harm,
He thought his next plan would work like a charm.

Job was cursed with sore boils on that day,
But he blessed his God, any ol' way.

Now even Job's wife pressed him the most,
To curse his God, and give up the Ghost.

And even his friends tried to cause him to sin.
But he was full of the Spirit and he did win.

Cause the Latter End of Job was truly blessed,
For the faith and trust he did possess.

So be like Job in your steadfast Love,
And receive your blessings from God above.

(Rap Style)

Dr. Lydia A. Woods

What's His Face?

Genesis 3:15; John 19:11 (KJV)

A very long time ago, so the Bible tells,
A foul rotten thing in heaven did dwell.

He was cast from heaven on that fateful day,
He fell to earth so the scriptures say.

And in his anger he began to plot and plan,
To get revenge on God's beloved Man.

In the garden of Eden he did beguile,
While deceiving Adam and Eve all the while.

Then Adam's power over the earth, he did take,
And from that day to this, war on man did make.

But almighty God was just a step ahead,
And sent His Word in the flesh, in man's stead.

In the flesh He came to save you and me,
They crucified Him so all could see.

And that's where the evil one made, his stupid mistake,
For the life of Jesus, he could not take.

Acceptance with Joy

'Cause no sin could be found in the Holy One,
The Lamb of God, His beloved Son.

That's when all of his power over you and me,
Was given back to our Savior, you see.

Now he walks around seeking to destroy,
Anyone who believes they are his toy.

But I'm, here to tell that no power exists
Over those who would only resist,

And claim Jesus as their Savior, the Holy One,
And believe in Him, their life has just begun.

So put him under foot, when he talks to you,
'Cause you're the Righteousness of God, tried and true.

And he's a thief, a liar and a big disgrace,
I can't remember his name, you know, "What's his face?"

For the Edification of the Saints

Dr. Lydia A. Woods

Adult vs Child

Matthew 18:3; Proverbs 22:6; Luke 18:16 (KJV)

As an adult, how many times have you thought?
In the good old days, I really had it made,
Mom and dad paid all of the bills,
I had it good, I had it made in the shade.

Now adulthood, is a relative term.
The world teaches you well indeed.
Everyone trying to get grown so fast,
Being responsible and planning to succeed.

That's what it takes in this world today,
A mature and responsible adult,
You'll have all of your dreams fulfilled,
But is that really the final result?

Why is it that the Father teaches,
Just the opposite of what the world sells,
To become as a little child....
Trusting in Him so you won't go to hell!

Now the author of kill, steal, and destroy,
Hates all of God's children; it's true,
He's mad as hell cause he can't inherit,
And I think he's just a little jealous, don't you?

So this adulthood is for the birds,
Go on, try being a child; there's no catch,
The Father wants all your troubles and cares,
Adult vs child - No Competition, not even a Match!

Dr. Lydia A. Woods

But For Your Praying Saints

Ephesians 6:18; I Thessalonians 5:17; James 5:16 (KJV)

Look out Satan cause you've been uncovered,
The truth has been told by my spiritual brother,
Frank Peretti is the Saint that's blessed me well.
He reveals what's going on in the pit of hell.

When he reads his book, "*This Present Darkness*" on cassette,
I'm telling you Saints you will never regret.
Listening to this book will spiritually educate you,
It will give you insight on just what to do.

His book is all about Satan's demons as they plot and plan,
To destroy God's Saints and steal the souls of man.
But don't despair the Lord's warriors are in place.
He dispatches angelic forces and they're on the case.

Their weapons are mighty for strongholds come down,
And they are powered by Saints that aren't playing around.
He speaks of Saints who know just what to do,
Using the power of prayer as they were commanded to.

Acceptance with Joy

As those mighty prayers ascend to the throne.
They empower the angels and they make right the wrong.
They can take out Satanic demons left and right,
They make quick work of them in this spiritual fight.

My daughter and I play the tape over and over again,
We love to hear the ending, when the angels win,
And then there's our favorite line in all of the book,
As the demon breathes his last and takes one long look,

At the captain of the host his angelic enemy,
Now here's the part that thrills my daughter and me.
Before he is vanquished – he speaks deep and faint,
But for your praying saints.........

Dr. Lydia A. Woods

Created in My Father's Image

Philippians 2:6; Galatians 4:6 (KJV)

If you see me you've seen my Father,
Though you and He may have never met.
I am the child of His seed,
I believe that He has no regrets,

For He knows that one day I will be,
A perfect reflection of Himself in me,

In so many ways I'm becoming like,
My Father that you do not see,
The way I think, behave, and speak,
It's amazing what He's doing in me.

He's laboring in love with me,
As the years of my growth go by,
Why He has cared, I may never know,
It may come clear before I die,

Or maybe sometime before then,
When my heart has been given away,
To the child of my very own seed,
I'll understand my Father's love that day.

Acceptance with Joy

It is the "Circle of Life," that just goes round,
For generations a marvelous plan,
The Lord wanted to share His greatest joy,
The Gift of Creation -- with His precious man.

Where would I be without my Father today?
This life He's made possible to me.
With love and security I have grown,
To be this person that you see.

I honor you Abba Father, not just today, but all my days,
Giving honor where honor is due.
Your child so humbly wants to express,
That her heart is full of love just for you!

Dr. Lydia A. Woods

Don't Envy Those

Malachi 3:13-18 (KJV)

Do not envy those that seem, to prosper in their way,
I quote this scripture to myself every day,

They all seem to be prospering, and I'm left behind,
Serving the Lord, and sorting everything out in my mind,

I understand with my head, that soon the wicked will be cut down,
And in that final day, the Lord will not be found,

I know that He's preparing, his people to stand in the evil day,
We're being tempered in the fire, that's the Lord's unique way.

But there are days when my mind, and emotions get in the way,
As they buy their material things, take trips, and then to me say,

"Oh, Lydia where are you going, for vacation this year",
Or "Why don't you just buy a house, don't rent.... you're losing money dear".

Acceptance with Joy

"Go on take out a loan, buy what your heart most desires,
Everybody is doing it, you know, it's what the world requires."

I sometimes get frustrated, and feel sorry for myself,
And then the Lord will show me, how blessed I am, by His wealth.

That He's blessed me so well, that I never should complain,
Then I want someone to kick me in the behind, because I feel so ashamed.

That I ever doubted His word, or murmured and complained,
I can't stand this flaw in myself, Lord please help me to change.

I can't change myself, even though I try every day,
I didn't make myself, I came into the world this way,

But I can cry out daily to the Father, to keep working on me,
For only He can make me like, his Son and from sin be free!

Dr. Lydia A. Woods

The Family Business

I Corinthians 3:7-9 (KJV)

So you've been called into the family,
Congratulations you're on your way,
Let me give you just a glimpse,
Of the Family Business as it stands today!

The Father has cattle on thousands of hills,
His fields are green and vast to view,
His wealth and family are beyond compare,
The Harvest is plentiful, but the workers are few.

I bet you didn't know of the family business,
Our business in growing and harvesting Souls,
The harvesting is constant and ongoing,
We harvest Souls from the young to the old.

Only the Father knows when they have ripened,
He's been in the business since the beginning of time,
Can you imagine the size of His wealth,
Just contemplating it blows your mind.

You see my brothers and sisters are all overworked,
Planting seeds and watering the fields,
The Father has mandated the tares grow with the wheat,
But it's the Father that determines the yields,

The Father wants every family member,
To be committed to the family goals,
Not going in their own direction,
But getting in the fields and harvesting those Souls.

A Compilation of Christian Poetry   For the Edification of the Saints

Acceptance with Joy

So if you haven't made that commitment,
Get with the Father for His plan for your life,
You'll find out that the pay and standard of living,
Can support a large family and even a wife!

The benefits far surpass any outside employment,
The health plan and insurance are absolutely free,
He has provided for all of your needs,
Talk to your many brothers and sisters and see!

Now in the beginning you start with the small jobs,
Your responsibilities increasing as you prove your worth,
But no matter the size of your job,
We all get paid the same, because of our birth.

I'm very proud of the family business,
Looking forward to new family members, to bring in that crop,
It gets hot in those fields and the work is tedious,
But quite rewarding and none of us, would ever think to stop.

Lift your head up with pride and don't tire,
Teach your children when they are young,
That the family business is where the future lies,
It's rewarding, never boring, and really quite fun!

Dr. Lydia A. Woods

Fear vs Faith

I John 4:18; Romans 8:15; Luke 12:32; Psalm 118:6 (KJV)

My beloved, the world teaches fear!
Your inheritance from time of old.
In the garden it entered in,
To this day fear wants to claim your soul.

When fear has its perfect work,
Sin is produced and the harvest is ripe.
And when sin is finally complete,
Then death comes and claims your spiritual life.

But the Father did not give that Spirit of fear,
You know who is the author of that!
Remember it's a spirit that comes and goes,
But you can rebuke it and that's a fact!

The Father gives us a measure of faith,
So work it and build it up very strong,
Like those outward bodies you work on so much,
Build that faith and you will never go wrong!

A Compilation of Christian Poetry   *For the Edification of the Saints*

Acceptance with Joy

Fighting fear is a daily steady routine,
'Cause the world taught you to fear so well,
But you can overcome this enemy,
That's trying to take your soul to hell.

Go on, walk in the faith that He's given,
You'll have plenty of trials to practice on,
Use that shield of faith, please the Father,
Watch fear take a hike and be gone!

Practice laughing in the face of fear,
Go on try faith, there's no catch.
You'll get better at it every day,
Fear vs Faith - No Competition, not even a Match!

Dr. Lydia A. Woods

Go the Distance

Revelation 2:1-29, 3:1-22 (KJV)

I like a good mystery,
I've read many in my time,
I work out the details
And plots in my mind.

Can't wait for the ending,
For the author to tell,
Just who is the bad guy
And who's going to jail!

Well the Bible is the best mystery,
That I ever read,
It keeps me on edge,
So many plots in my head.

But I wouldn't get caught,
Not reading the end,
Cause to a mystery hound like me,
That's really an unforgivable sin.

So it really amazes me,
How so many can resist,
Reading the last chapter,
And all that good ending miss.

Even the name of that chapter,
Rings quite true,
"Revelation" reveals the whole book,
To me and to you.

Acceptance with Joy

The author was clever,
For not all can see,
The final outcome,
Of this amazing mystery!

So I'll reveal a little truth,
That few know,
Just what the overcomer receives,
When the distance they go.

For the race is not given,
To the swift or the strong,
But he that endures to the end,
Will never go wrong.

Now I found that the overcomer,
Will eat of the tree of life,
That tree in the garden,
Denied to Adam and his wife.

The overcomer will eat hidden manna,
Receive a stone of pure white,
A new name in that stone,
So John, the author, writes.

The overcomer gets power,
To rule over the nations,
Given by the Morning Star,
For the overcomer has learned His patience.

Dr. Lydia A. Woods

White raiment is given ,
To show that we are pure,
Our name in the Book of Life,
Of that you can be sure.

Before the Father,
Our Savior confesses our name,
Also to the Angels in Heaven,
Our triumph proclaim.

A Pillar in the Temple of God,
We'll stand tall and straight,
Bearing the Name of our God,
And His city, I can hardly wait.

Our Lord's new name will be written,
On us for all to see,
Sealed there forever,
Unto all eternity.

So go the distance,
And never faint or fear,
For your Salvation is at hand,
And Redemption is near.

Last, but not least,
The Lord has granted to thee,
To sit with Him in His throne,
Forever Saved and Free!

Dr. Lydia A. Woods

God Will Provide

Genesis 22:1-19 (KJV)

For in Isaac shall thy seed be called,
And this Seed the one to save us all.

But it came to pass, God called to Abraham,
Behold, "Here I am, Lord what is your command.?

Sacrifice Isaac thy only son to Me,
Take him to a place I will show to thee.

Lay him on an altar a burnt offering make,
Abraham rose, only his son and provision did take.

Isaac inquired of his father and this is why,
Abraham said to Isaac – "my son, here am I."

Isaac said, "Behold, there is fire and wood,
But we need a lamb to make this offering good."

For the burnt offering where is the lamb,
Tell me this – my father Abraham?

A Compilation of Christian Poetry   *For the Edification of the Saints*

Acceptance with Joy

God will provide himself a lamb, Abraham said,
Then he bound his only son to that altar bed.

He took the knife stretched forth his hand,
To slay his son – that was God's command.

Then the angel of the Lord called unto him,
Abraham, Abraham stay your hand my friend.

Here am I, your servant, what is thy Will?
The Angel said, I know now that you love God still.

Abraham turned – a ram was caught by his horns,
He called the place Jehovah Jireh on that morn.

Because he did not withhold the thing he loved,
Many blessings flowed from God above.

And in thy seed shall all nations be blessed,
God will Provide! – Every saint can attest!

Dr. Lydia A. Woods

Group Three

Matthew 8:12, 13:37-43; Luke 13:24-30 (KJV)

I'm very, very concerned about those in group three,
Because this group feels they are saved and free,
I was a member of that group for many years,
That group lives in deception and has many fears.

The deception of this group is enormous indeed,
They profess to living by God's Holy creed,
They profess to knowing the Father and Son,
They profess to Salvation but they have none,

They go to church, some since their birth,
They think they'll go to heaven when they leave this earth,
They have never experienced a Spiritual moment with Christ,
There really is no relationship, but only sin in their life.

They are in denial about their relationship with God.
They front, 'cause they don't want others to think them odd,
It's the going thing, you know, in this day and age,
Dressing up, and attending church is all the rage.

They go to the big church on the corner, for all to see,
Or the medium or small church, it's a religious decree,
They have their activities and programs galore,
And the building programs that will give them more.

More rooms and space so that activities can grow,
It's a sad religious existence, I want you to know.
Because they are only fooling themselves,
As they pursue their illusions and gather their wealth,

Acceptance with Joy

For in that final day as they stand at the door,
The Lord will open and they will implore,
Entrance to His Holy place,
But He will not know their names or recognize their face.

He will say I never, ever knew you,
Because you didn't do, what I asked you to.
You had many plans and ways of your own,
But I was not a part of them, look at the seeds you've sown.

Now who are those that are in group two?
It's filled with sinners, not saved, what about you?
They know they live in sin and are lost as can be,
But group one is the light of the world, to help them see,

And of course group one are the children of God,
A peculiar people indeed – and kind of odd,
Living as examples of Christ, for all to know,
That God is real and loves them so.

So in group three, you're just a wanna-be,
Pretending to know the Lord, bound and not free.
Stumbling around, puffed up in self-righteousness and fear,
Recognize your sins today,
Group one will be praying for you all my dears!

Dr. Lydia A. Woods

Hedge of Protection

Psalm 91:1-16; I Peter 3:4-6 (KJV)

You have placed your hedge of protection,
Around me tight as a drum,
No one can penetrate through it,
No, not anyone....

Within your hedge of protection,
Our relationship grows strong every day,
You're preparing me for my future,
This vessel you'll use in your special way.

I feel safe and warm in your hedge,
I can look out on the world and see,
All the men and women and their relationships,
They're in trouble and that once was me.

I once operated outside the Father,
In relationships made on my own,
Wreaking havoc in the lives of others,
Now I'm reaping what I have sown.

There's no fleshly feelings or burning,
For your hedge provides perfect peace,
And in my celibacy, I sometimes wonder,
When your hedge of protection will cease.

Lord I pray that Your hedge of protection,
Stays round me until the season comes,
For me to join with the mate You've selected,
And You and he and I become one.

Dr. Lydia A. Woods

How Many Times

Philippians 4:19 (KJV)

How many times must I,
Snatch you from the jaws of the devourer,
For you to remember,
That I am there for you hour after hour.

How many times must I,
Meet your need,
For you to remember,
That you are my lamb that I will feed.

How many times must I,
Surprise you with the secrets of your heart,
For you to remember,
That it is sweet gifts to you that I wish to impart.

How many times must I,
Comfort you,
For you to remember,
That I will always be there to rescue.

How many times must I,
Bless your children,
For you to remember,
That I will carry your every burden.

Acceptance with Joy

How many times must I,
Put food on your table,
For you to remember,
That I will never forsake - I am more than able.

How many times must I,
Pay your bills,
For you to remember,
That to provide for you is my divine will.

How many times must I,
Keep you and your children in health,
For you to remember,
That My Son took your sickness onto Himself.

How many times before you will believe,
That I love you,
I will pursue you until you know,
That it is true.

Look back and count,
All that I have done,
I have blessed you so many times,
You can't remember every one.

Dr. Lydia A. Woods

When revelation knowledge comes to you,
Of my endless love,
Then you can move from this grievous place,
And I'll lift you far above,

The day to day pressures of this world,
Filled with fear and strife,
And greater things I can accomplish,
Through your precious life.

So remember when the enemy speaks to you,
Do what my Son taught you to,

Say, "It is written Satan, you have no power here".
Speak the Word with boldness and never fear,
That I will not honor my own Word when I hear.

How many times - they are endless, My Dear.

How Will I Know Him?

Genesis 24:1-67 (KJV)

Many young girls ask their mothers,
Just how will I know I'm in love?
After many failed relationships and wounded heart,
I asked this question, of my Father above.

He said, "Not as the world giveth,
Select I a mate just for you,
A mate that's prepared and rooted in me,
Washed in my Blood, a creature brand new."

"How will I know him?" I asked the Father,
His reply was simple indeed,
"By his spirit, my dear, you can tell,
If he's in Me and born of My Seed.

His outer appearance won't move you,
This is not a matter of flesh,
The gentleness and love in his heart,
You'll want to forever caress.

The joining of our spirits,
Yours and his and Mine,
A perfect union made by My hand,
To be bound in the Spirit for all time.

His spirit will witness to you,
The heart of the man I will reveal,
You'll love his love of the Father,
And in our love your union, I'll seal."

Dr. Lydia A. Woods

I Need the Eyes of Jesus

Luke 4:18; Psalm 119:105; I Corinthians 3:16 (KJV)

Oh how I long to see – me, with Jesus' precious eyes
For so long I have been blind, using Satan for my guide,

Satan tells me to step down; when it's up that I should go.
He tells me I am unattractive,
When I am clothed with light and glow,

He says that I am helpless, when power is in my hand,
He tells me I am crippled, when I only need to stand.

He says I will not make it,
When Jesus has already overcome,
He says, I've lost the fight, when I've only just begun.

He says that I will never,
Become the perfection in Jesus Christ,
He says that I'm a loser, and that he will take my life.

The blinders cover my eyes, so that truth will hide from sight,
They need only be removed
To make my vision quite alright.

Satan seeks not only, to kill, steal and destroy,
But blinding God's children, is the basis of his ploy.

Acceptance with Joy

I can hardly bear the light,
For my eyes are darkened inside this shell,
But without the vision you possess,
I will be defeated and end in hell.

I do not want to stumble and fall,
So give me vision for my task,
You said, I only had to knock,
Or only need to ask.

I'm asking you today,
To unlock the blindness, set me free,
Jesus make these blind eyes open,
I know you are the only key.

Your vast and wonderful greatness,
Inside my vessel I want to see,
I need the eyes of Jesus,
For my true self to be revealed to me.

Dr. Lydia A. Woods

If You Want to Make God Laugh!

Proverbs 19:21; Matthew 5:36; Isaiah 46:9-11 (KJV)

The old folk used to say, "It's all in God's Hands,"
And if you want to make God laugh,
Just tell Him your plans!

That you're gonna do this and that,
You're over twenty-one and that's a fact,
You're big and bad, so much in control,
Do what you want 'cause you're grown and bold.

The world taught you well about the planning part,
Everybody does it, and that's being smart.
To become a responsible adult and grown,
You must get on the go, get a plan of your own.

The sooner you realize that you have no power,
To make things happen from hour to hour,
That you can't change one hair on your head,
That you didn't wake yourself up today to get out of bed.

That you're a little child who can't come in or go out,
It doesn't do any good to get mad or even pout.
Things are out of your control so get with the plan,
That everything is purposed by God's own hand.

Acceptance with Joy

You were bought with a price
Do you know just what that means,
You got to give it up,
No use making a childish scene.

Scripture says, "Many are the plans of a man,
But God's purposes will prevail throughout the land,"
Stop drowning in the sea of denial,
'Cause you're bound to Him all the while.

So if you want to make God laugh today,
Just open your mouth, let Him hear you say,
That you've got plans and you're gonna do this and that,
Watch the Hand of God just slap you Back!

Dr. Lydia A. Woods

In a Split Second

James 1:8; II Corinthians 10:5 (KJV)

In a split second your mind,
Can conjure up disaster,
And your demise comes from,
The great deceiving master.

When trouble comes,
Your mind is as active as can be,
Ripe for the picking,
And panic sets in so thoroughly.

You have a vivid imagination,
That can lead you to the grave,
You worry and stress yourself out,
And then begin to behave,

Like a stressed out nut,
Running here and running there,
Your weight goes up or down,
Then you begin to lose your hair.

You live and feed on fear,
And that's your daily bread,
It's amazing all the scenarios,
That you are playing out in your head.

Acceptance with Joy

If you look back and count,
What never came to be,
You will realize that the Word of God,
Can set you free.

Free from worry and stress,
And every evil work,
Free from your own thoughts,
That can drive you berserk.

Cast down those vain imaginings,
That come into your head,
Satan puts them there because,
He wants to see you dead.

So stop this foolish worrying,
It will only shorten your life span,
Commit your future to the Lord,
Place yourself within His hand.

"Don't worry, be happy,"
As the songwriter* wrote one day,
Tell Satan to take a hike,
And pack his bags, be on his way.

Dr. Lydia A. Woods

And in that split second,
When panic takes you to your doom,
Change your perspective, keep the faith,
For faith rids you of the gloom.

After you cast down those vain imaginings,
This is what you do,
Apply the Word of God, to your situation,
As you were commanded to.

Believe what the Word says,
It's not based on how good you are,
But on God's Grace and Mercy,
And His Righteousness...By Far!

* "Don't Worry, Be Happy." by Bobby McFerrin

Dr. Lydia A. Woods

The Inside of the Cup

Matthew 23:25; Luke 11:39 (KJV)

Hypocrites, vipers, in your fine array,
Dressed to the hilt strutting your stuff today.

All in your finery going to worship your God,
Sitting on those pews, to me you look quite odd.

For are we reading, the same Bible, you and me,
For I have looked and looked, but I just don't see.

I do read that the traditions of man choke the Word,
And in man's traditions the Word just cannot be heard.

The Word warns us not to take heed to the cup's outside,
But tend to the cleanliness inside where the spirit abides.

It is the world that has taught you to look your best,
But by outward appearance, you can never pass the Lord's test.

Acceptance with Joy

Look deeper my precious Saints, inside the inner man,
And you will find spirits that are weak, emaciated and bland.

Spirits that are starving, needing to be spiritually fed,
Even though the outward body looks healthy, not even near dead.

But it is near death, that they are in reality, you see,
God's reality is far above you and me.

But we can access the mind, of the living Christ,
By the gift of love that He gave, when He paid the price.

Take your cup for a cleansing, on the inside every day,
Now it's only His blood, that can clean it in such a way,

That can get out all stains, dirt, grease and grime,
Don't be deceived precious saints. No, Not this Time!

Dr. Lydia A. Woods

It's Not About Money

Luke 12:22-34; Matthew 6:25-34 (KJV)

Oh! I'm finally really getting it,
I'm kind of a slow learner you see,
It's not about having a lot of money,
But putting my trust in thee,

It rains on the just and unjust,
Equally rain falls into every life,
But it's how you deal with the problems,
How you handle the grief and the strife.

Now everyone is feeling the pressure,
Life is stressful and everyone is running scared.
But do you have a place to run to,
When everyone else is losing their head?

I'm learning not to lose my cool,
When things seem to be going all astray,
It happens so often that I'm beginning to wonder,
Maybe this is just the norm for life today.

The Lord wants me to rely on Him,
Not on money to solve every ill,
It's not money I really need,
Because trust in the Lord is a better deal.

It's finally sinking into my thick skull,
The years of trial and tribulation is creating in me,
The ability to be lifted to a higher level,
Of Trust and Rest and Peace in thee....

Dr. Lydia A. Woods

Oh! To be Like the Master

John 8:12, 28-29, 31 (KJV)

Oh! How I long to be like the Master,
Just think of how He carried Himself,
With a confidence and an assurance,
Of who He was, and of His Father's wealth.

It was this calm and peaceful demeanor,
The air of royalty and perfect peace,
That drew multitudes to listen so intently,
To Words that they hoped would never cease.

Now the Master was cool,
He had His act together,
For He knew who He was,
And what the Father would do.

He never doubted,
But spoke words filled with faith,
The Words of His Father,
As He has commanded - Us to.

At the wedding feast,
They all got anxious,
His mother, Mary asked Him to help out,
She was His mom, and didn't have a doubt.

He didn't break a sweat,
As he commanded them to fill,
All those jugs with water,
How they marveled at the Master's skill.

A Compilation of Christian Poetry   *For the Edification of the Saints*

Acceptance with Joy

Now the sisters, Mary and Martha,
Were extremely upset,
Brother Lazarus had died,
And they had only, one regret,

That if the Master had been there,
He would not have died,
And they were in His face,
Wanting to know just why?

Why, had it taken Him so long,
To come to their heed,
For Lazarus was already decaying,
In the tomb, now there was no need.

The Master prayed to the Father,
For everyone to behold,
"Lazarus come forth" He spoke,
The Word strong and bold.

Now the Master was cool,
He had His act together,
He knew who He was,
And what the Father would do.

He never doubted,
But spoke words filled with faith,
The Words of His Father,
As He has commanded - Us to.

Dr. Lydia A. Woods

Those disciples worried,
And fear took them in that boat,
While the Master slept,
Things would be calm if He were woke.

So in panic they awaken Him,
To come to their aid,
He calmed the rain and the wind,
And then to them did bade.

Why did you trouble me?
Where was your faith?
How long must I suffer,
To teach you to live by God's good grace?

Know who you are in the Father,
And what He will do,
Be skillful in the Word,
That I am teaching you.

The people were all worried,
About the woman who had sinned.
Took her to the Master,
For Him to condemn.

But He just calmly asked, of their own sin,
And wrote in the sand,
They all dropped their stones,
And walked away – every man.

Acceptance with Joy

Now the Master was cool,
He had His act together,
For He knew who He was,
And what the Father would do.

He never doubted,
But spoke words filled with faith,
The Words of His Father,
As He has commanded – Us to.

The man came to the Master,
Cause his daughter was dying,
When the Master showed up,
they were weeping and crying.

For the daughter had died,
and they laughed at Him,
When He said she only slept,
They thought Him quite dim.

He commanded,
That everyone leave,
Into the house with faith,
In His Father He believed,

Then He commanded,
That she rise and be fed,
He blew their minds,
And this played with their heads

Dr. Lydia A. Woods

Now the Master was cool,
He had His act together,
He knew who He was,
And what the Father would do.

He never doubted,
But spoke words filled with faith,
The Words of His Father,
As He has commanded - Us to.

Oh! How I long to be like the Master,
It's badly needed today,
I want to emulate His confidence
And faith in such a way,

That I live up to the work He started,
Here on earth is the Master's trust,
And through His precious Holy Spirit,
That He has graciously placed - In us.

Oh! To be like the Master, we just Must!

Dr. Lydia A. Woods

Somethin' Told Me

John 12:26; Ephesians 4:30; Luke 2:26 (KJV)

Somethin' told me,
I should have turned left when I turned right,
Somethin' told me,
I should have called her late last night,

Somethin' told me,
Not to say those unkind words,
Somethin' told me,
That my bill was due on the third,

Somethin' told me,
That you were not doing so well,
Somethin' told me,
That I could get that dress at the mall on sale,

Somethin' told me,
Not to pick up that phone or go into that room,
Somethin' told me,
That he wasn't the right bridegroom.

If I had a dollar,
For all the times I've heard,
But did not heed the gentle voice,
Or the light, urging, words,

Acceptance with Joy

Of the faint and fleeting sound,
Within my being,
Somethin' told me,
Without my knowing or my seeing.

The Somethin' told me,
One day not long ago,
Will you stop saying,
"Somethin'" told you so and so.

My name is not "Somethin',"
Please call my name out right,
My name is Holy Spirit,
And I live within you out of sight.

I was sent by my Master,
To lead and guide you into truth,
My job is to protect you,
Bring you to remembrance. Do you need proof?

Just open up my Word,
And read about Me for yourself,
My name is not "Somethin',"
But I'm your Lord – It's Me Myself!

Dr. Lydia A. Woods

Take a Visit to the Upper Room

Acts 1:3-4, 8, 2:1-21 (KJV)

Have you ever visited the upper room?
Don't want to get in your business or assume,
That everyone knows just where it's at,
So let me lay it out in white and black.

Jesus told those disciples to go to that place,
Don't go anywhere else, to the room make haste.
For you can't witness or testify effectively,
Until the Holy Ghost comes, and gets in thee.

For you need special Power from on High,
To be successful in the fight and this is why,
Jesus got the Holy Ghost too, before the wilderness,
He battled with Satan, and He did effectively resist.

So how do you think you can do battle too,
If the Holy Spirit doesn't get in you?
When the Holy Spirit came down on Jesus like a dove,
Didn't God say, "This is my Son, my beloved!"

It takes Power from on High to walk down here,
To do battle with the enemy and have no fear,
To speak of what is written and to use the Name,
Of Jesus Christ the Savior you have claimed.

John the Baptist spoke from his own mouth,
That there was one to come that would bring about.
Not the water baptism of repenting from sin,
But Baptism with the Holy Ghost, and fire only from Him.

Acceptance with Joy

You're not done when you receive the Savior,
Go just one step further, do yourself a favor,
Ask the Lord for what He has promised,
Don't be caught being a doubting Thomas!

Don't just stop halfway through,
There is so much more the Lord has for you!

But it's not automatic you have to ask to receive,
You have to have faith and in Him believe,
That he will place His Holy Spirit in you,
A new creature to be born, with work to do.

He wants you to have Power from on High,
He wants to give you a new tongue and this is why,
That new tongue edifies only you,
It's a part of being reborn, becoming brand new.

Praying in the Spirit He commands every day,
It builds your faith, it's just the Lord's way.
I didn't make this up, it's all in the book,
Don't y'all go giving me that funny look.

The Holy Spirit wants to use your voice,
So give Him His way, come on, make that choice.
The Lord wants you to practice decreasing yourself,
As the Spirit increases and you partake of his wealth,

Dr. Lydia A. Woods

The Lord takes the foolish things of men to confound the wise,
Do not try to make sense of it or justify,
'Cause your intellect will get in the way,
And you can't receive what the Lord has for you today.

Only the sincere in heart that wants to receive,
With a childlike nature and a spirit that dares to believe,
That God will do His thing, and it will be alright,
He never needed to ask our advice.

So when the Holy Spirit wants those gifts to come out,
You'll get out the way and won't have a doubt.
That the Holy Spirit is ready to work through you,
To edify the Body or cast out -- you know who.

So go to the upper room, don't tarry dear,
Many have gone before, so have no fear,
I tell you these things so that you will be blessed,
And I won't be like John, crying in the wilderness.

Dr. Lydia A. Woods

The Time is Short!

Mark 13:20; Acts 1:7; I Thessalonians 5:1-2; II Peter 3 (KJV)

The time must be shortened, so the scripture say,
For even the elect could be deceived in that day,

That latter day when the spirit of antichrist is full,
And sinners and saints have forgotten the golden rule.

To love one another, as He has loved us,
To give Him our hearts and in Him only trust.

The way is not straight and only He can be our guide,
Put your reasoning and thinking to the side,

For you cannot walk the straightway with the sight in your eyes,
Ask for understanding and wisdom; let it be your guide,

And that wisdom is found, in His Holy Spirit, you know,
Jesus left Him here to help show us the way to go.

Acceptance with Joy

He will lead you home, through this world of sin,
Without the Holy Spirit's help, you can never win,

That race that is given, only to them that endure,
With His guidance don't worry, your victory is sure.

Hurry my brothers and sisters, you I implore,
Come quickly through that tiny open Door,

Choose the Lord this day, while He may be found,
Stop wasting precious time just fooling around.

The time is short, the signs tell us day by day,
Listen, I beg you, to what I have to say,
Is my job truly hopeless, will "not anyone hear?
The Word said, In the latter days
They won't bear sound teaching," I fear!

Dr. Lydia A. Woods

Was He Saved? Did He Know the Lord?

John 13:34-35; I John 4:21 (KJV)

When my father died,
My Christian friends asked me,
"Was he saved?
Did he know the Lord?"

I replied,

"I never heard him say he was a Christian,
I never heard him pray out loud,
He never went to church on Sunday,
While serving Jesus all the while.

He lived what Jesus commanded,
Never an unkind word that he spoke,
Loving his brother and sister in all his ways,
So humble in spirit did his manner denote.

He was a humble servant to many,
He was blessed all of his days,
I just marvel at the fruit he produced,
As he modeled Christ in his everyday ways.

I saw him pour out his life for others,
He never turned a man from his door,
He was filled with a knowing wisdom,
He had a heart and mind to explore.

And in that wisdom he never spoke of his faith,
Although he lived it in all of his ways,
There was never a doubt in my mind,
That he knew the Lord or was saved."

A Compilation of Christian Poetry   For the Edification of the Saints

Acceptance with Joy

What is the greatest commandment,
That in doing you cover all the rest?
Love the Lord thy God with all thy
Heart, mind, soul and strength,
Love your brother as yourself and no less.

The heart of a man we will never know,
For that is given to the Lord,
But scripture tells us to try every spirit,
Using the Word like a two-edged sword.

The Bible reports that Jesus will say to many,
In the last days, I never knew you,
You never lived as I commanded,
You never did what I asked you to!

Look at the life of a man or woman,
Look at the fruit upon the tree,
Check for signs of full growth and ripeness,
It tells the truth of that person, you see.

Another person's Salvation,
Is between them and our Father above,
Let the Spirit bear witness and the Angels record,
"Was he saved? – Did He Know the Lord?"

Food for Saints

Dr. Lydia A. Woods

Above All

John 14:13; I John 5:14; Ephesians 3:10 (KJV)

Why is it written that He will do,
Above all that we ask Him to?

Also above that which we can think, also,
I've often wondered about this, I want to know.

I've figured out that He's placed every desire in my heart,
That it did not originate on my small part.

The Lord placed those desires so long ago,
Before I was born in fact – didn't you know?

So if He has placed those desires there,
He is also able to fulfill them with love and care.

But He holds a little back for Himself,
To surprise His children and bless them with His wealth.

Acceptance with Joy

That's the part about "Above All," that we can think or ask,
He saves the extra special part until the very last.

He has wealth, that even our minds can't comprehend,
And He likes to play the "Above Card," in the end.

He enjoys seeing our joy and delight,
It makes our testimony glorious and extraordinarily bright.

We can't wait to tell just what He has done,
We want to run and share it with everyone.

That He didn't just do, what we had asked,
But He went beyond that wee small task.

He never does things tiny or infinitely small,
But He is in the business of – Above All!

Dr. Lydia A. Woods

Be Still!

Psalm 46:10 (KJV)

As a child of God, He often says to me,
Child "Be Still," just wait and see.
I hate it when He says, "Be Still,"
Cause' my flesh is jumpin' – that's against my will.

He means, "Be Still," in your flesh and mouth and mind,
Just sit yourself down on your behind.

The nature of a child is to move, move about,
Running here and there trying to figure things out.
Just what to do about this and that,
That's true about kids and that is just a fact.

So when the Father says to "Be Still,"
He means that we are to submit our Will,
The very thing that you want to do,
Put it on the shelf, like He told you to.

He has a plan for the problem already in hand,
Before you were born, because He "Is the Man,"
In heaven and earth it's always His Will,
So will you just sit down and "Be Still!"

Dr. Lydia A. Woods

Children of the King

I John 3:1, 9; Psalm 91:11; Matthew 4:6 (KJV)

Do you really know how the children of Kings are treated?
They are waited on hand-and-foot while they are seated.

And when they get up to walk about,
The servants clear a path without a doubt.

Preparation is always being made on their behalf,
They are never far from the king's rod or staff.

Maybe the example of "Children of Kings," is too far out for you,
Let me bring it closer to home for your review.

Now the President of the United States has secret service guys,
And what is their purpose? – I will tell you why.

They are sent before to scout out the situation,
To make sure it's safe, posting men at every station.

Undercover secret service are everywhere,
Assassins watch out – you are stupid if you dare,

To attack the President would not be very wise.
It's a crazy scary plan that I would not advise.

A Compilation of Christian Poetry   *Food for Saints*

Acceptance with Joy

'Cause the secret service will be on you, like white on rice,
They won't treat you kindly or handle you very nice.

The President is important and special indeed,
For the nation to function and thrive and succeed.

And God's children are special and important in this dark hour,
He plans for us to succeed, as we walk with pride and power.

Now imagine, that your secret service people are on the job,
Get a sense that what I'm saying isn't so very odd.

Our undercover agents are Angels you know,
They are around you and above you - wherever you go.

They've been assigned by the Father to protect His child,
Keeping you guarded and safe on earth, all the while.

Surely goodness and mercy will follow you all of your days,
This is just another example of our loving Father's ways.

Get a revelation – blessed children of the King,
Begin to walk with pride and boldness into Anything!

Doin' the Adam

Genesis 3:1-24 (KJV)

Now I want you to check Genesis out,
Because everyone seems to believe,
That Adam was away in the garden,
Not standing beside his wife Eve.

When the serpent began his conversation,
Lying and twisting God's Holy Word.
Tempting Eve of the fruit to partake,
The whole conversation Adam surely heard.

It was Adam that God gave dominion,
Over the earth and every living new birth,
All he needed to say to the serpent was,
Be gone – I cast you out from the earth.

But he abdicated his authority,
He sold his very birthright,
His power over the earth was given to Satan,
Now Satan ruled over Adam and his wife.

They lost their glorified bodies,
They became subject to death that day,
This hindered their relationship with God,
Because they listened to what Satan had to say.

Acceptance with Joy

Why did he not use his authority?
Why did he stand stupidly by?
Did he not understand his commission, from the Lord?
Can anyone tell me why?

And if you can tell why Adam,
Committed that sin long ago,
Then you can probably tell me why Saints today,
Are doin' the Adam and don't seem to know,

That God carried out a glorious plan,
To restore us to Himself through His Son.
Giving all power back in the hands of the Saints,
By the victory that Jesus won.

So don't be caught doin' the Adam,
I see Saints falling for Satan's old familiar song,
Don't stand stupidly by and listen,
Remember – Adam's mistake, now make right the wrong!

Dr. Lydia A. Woods

Father Knows Best

Proverbs 1:7; James 1:5 (KJV)

"Father Knows Best," was the name of a television show,
I know I'm dating myself, but some of you know.

The wife and kids would get themselves in a stew,
But the wise Father always knew just what to do.

I know you've heard that where there's a will – there is a way.
I just want to discuss that old saying with you today.

For where our Will is, I only know there is a mess,
'Cause only the Will of the Father is the One that's best.

We try very hard to have our own way,
Telling God how it's going to be today.

Strutting around with our chests poked out,
We even have a nerve to get mad or pout.

But you know just what I'm talking about,
Look at your life the proof will bear me out.

Acceptance with Joy

That our will is the source of all the hurt and pain,
It has screwed us up – it can drive us insane.

I know that my will has got to lay down and die,
But it keeps getting up and this is why,

'Cause that will has been trained by the evil one,
To rebel against God and His precious Son.

The greatest gift the Lord gives is our own will,
But it's a difficult thing to make it be still.

To line it up with the Lord's, is the secret of life,
And living on this earth without fear or strife.

A will submitted to Him will find joy, peace and rest,
It's for our own good, 'cause, "Father Knows Best."

Dr. Lydia A. Woods

For the Elect's Sake

Mark 13:20 (KJV)

Have you noticed that the days,
Seem shorter and shorter each year,
Before you know it the months have flown,
Everyone's talking about time – now hear,

Just what is really going on,
With the time and why is it moving with speed?
Can you not discern the signs of the times,
Lend an ear to God's Word, give heed.

We are definitely in the last days,
Prophecy is fulfilling itself as I speak,
The spirit of antichrist is fully in season,
Many Saints today are just Spiritually weak.

He is shortening the days,
For the sake of the very Elect,
Because of the rampant sin,
In the world and the Elect doesn't really suspect,

That they are compromising God's Word,
They have a form of godliness but deny,
The power of His Name,
They are missing His commission and this is why.

Acceptance with Joy

They are attending church in great numbers,
Their itching ears heap teachers to themselves.
They are building great monuments and structures,
They marvel at the size of their congregations and their wealth.

But…
The Body of Christ by the Holy Spirit,
Is to be a powerful force in the world today,
But they won't take in His Holy Spirit,
That gives them power to defeat Satan in every way.

They are not walking in this power,
Doing greater things than the Lord did when He was here,
For their faith is extremely weak,
So much of the church in darkness and fear.

They fear the power of the Holy Spirit,
They won't let the gifts operate in their midst,
They are steeped in their traditions,
The ways of the Lord they resist.

Strongholds are not being broken,
People gather but none are set free.
Why do you continue to meet on Sunday
And never access the power in Me?

Dr. Lydia A. Woods

Bring your sick and heavy ladened,
To My altar, anoint them and lay hands in My Name,
Cast the demons out of the people,
Free their minds that Satan has claimed.

Believe in the power of My Name,
Use it boldly and never fear,
That My Word will return to Me void,
Are you listening my precious dears?

I have shortened the time for My Elect,
Satan seems to be winning, but My dears don't fear.
For those of you that are in Me,
Know that the victory is already here!

Dr. Lydia A. Woods

Get in the House

Exodus 12:12-14; James 2:12, 18-19 (KJV)

When you were young, outside you'd play,
And after a very long hard day.
When night was falling, mom would always say,
"Get in the House, play is over for today."

There is safety in the house when darkness falls,
So obey your mother when she calls,
Also obey the Heavenly Father's Word,
'Cause the plague is still lurking, so I've heard.

And so it was in days long ago,
The plague wandered in the streets – don't you know,
But all of Goshen land was spared,
For out the house they did not dare.

They spread the Blood above the door,
Obeyed the Father who evened the score,
With the Egyptians on that terrible day,
'Cause they didn't heed what Moses had to say.

"Let the people go," was the Father's command,
And against the Lord can no man stand,
Not even Pharaoh the mighty king,
Could save the first born from this thing.

Acceptance with Joy

There is salvation in the house for all inside,
It takes only one righteous for the others to abide.
That one righteous soul can cover a multitude of sin.
And win the salvation of all their house in the end.

The scriptures tell of other houses spared,
Because Noah listened to God and he did dare.
To build the Ark – then in it his family place,
And they all were saved by the Lord's good grace.

Now Rahab too made sure her family was within,
For she hid the spies and that covered her sin.
That red thread hung outside for all to see,
Symbolic of the Blood of Christ, who sets us free.

So get in the house for salvation is there,
For you and your household take special care.
You're commanded to cover it very well,
With the Lord's Blood, like a precious veil.

And He is faithful to save those gathered inside,
Never fear or fret it's for you to decide,
So remember what your mama used to say,
"Get in the House, play is over for today!"

Dr. Lydia A. Woods

God's M.O.

I Corinthians 1:26-27, 2:7, 3:19; Luke 2:7; Ephesians 3:5 (KJV)

My relationship with the Father,
Is growing from day to day,
I'm learning of His unique character,
And a little something about His way.

How He doesn't come right at you,
He's not in your face plain and clear.
But you need to look a little deeper,
To see what's really going on here.

How he brought His Son in low estate,
Not a King upon a throne,
He is subtle and quite ingenious,
But if you're not careful you'll go wrong.

He takes the foolishness of man,
To confound the very wise,
Those discarded things of man,
Are the Lord's greatest prize.

The very thing that doesn't appeal to you,
And makes you want to run the other way,
Give it a second deeper look,
Cause I discovered a secret one day.

Acceptance with Joy

That Satan comes at you like an angel of light,
Disguising the bad behind the good,
And the minute you take the bait,
That's when he pulls the hood,

And uncovers the horrible mess,
That he has sucked you in for sure,
Now you're screaming for help,
Looking to God for the problem's cure.

So don't be sucked in by outward appearances,
Listen carefully and look for God's M.O.
If it doesn't appeal to your flesh,
It's probably the way you ought to go.

So when I am just plain obedient,
Even when I don't want to obey,
I'm always fantastically blessed,
When I give in and do it God's way.

Dr. Lydia A. Woods

I'm Not Lucky – I'm Blessed!

Genesis 12:3, 26:4; Deuteronomy 7:3-14 (KJV)

I tell people all the time,
I'm not lucky – I'm blessed.
Luck is a word the world uses,
But blessed is the term I prefer to confess.

Lucky is not in the vocabulary of God's Word,
Saints rid luck from your conversation today.
It's only God's grace and mercy,
That follows us as we journey in life's way.

Lucky is a term of Satan,
It involves witchcraft and chances of fate.
But promises of God's blessings to His children,
Is not magic, but a sure and solid mandate.

We live in the showering of His blessings,
We walk in grace and mercy from hour to hour,
Miracles are just everyday occurrences,
It's our birthright to live our lives in His power.

The power of His Word,
That transcends every wicked device,
There is power in our tongues,
Saints let's correct our speech, that's my advice.

Remember that it is not luck,
That comes and goes at Satan's whim,
But the state of our existence,
When we walk by Faith in Him.

Dr. Lydia A. Woods

I'm Tired!

John 16:33; Ephesians 5:3-5 (KJV)

My precious Saints don't pray to be released,
Calling for the debt and troubles to cease.
Stop waiting for your ship to come in,
Falling for every scam of the enemy... Satan!

You know the familiar phrases you love to hear,
"The Lord doesn't want you in poverty my dear,"
"The Lord wants you to prosper," and I have a way,
Listen to this "Prosperity message," I'm selling today.

Don't fall for Satan's old funky tricks, that crook,
He uses the Word just enough to get you hooked.
You are so desperate to be out of debt,
Saints are tired of struggling of that you can bet.

You say...

I'm tired of not having money in the bank,
I'm tired of not having a brand new car with a full tank.
I'm tired of not Traveling here and there,
I'm tired of not having fancy clothes to wear.

I'm tired of this old boring job,
I'm tired of being peculiar and thought of as odd.
I'm tired of not having what I deserve,
I'm a child of God, haven't you heard?

Acceptance with Joy

He wants all His children to be prosperous you see,
So I'll just pray for what I want to come to me.
I know the Lord loves me so,
This can't be His plan for my life don't you know.

The debt and pressure and stress and strain,
It's all becoming too much for my little brain,
I'm really about to lose it Lord,
Where is all the prosperity you promised in Your Word?

It's all part of His plan for us,
Debt and tribulation are for a greater purpose.
To draw you closer and closer to Himself,
Making you rely on Him and His infinite wealth.

For His children have access to a greater wealth,
The Lord wants you to learn to access it for yourself,
Now I want to say this loud and clear,
Open up your ears so that you can hear.

The Lord wants you to rely and trust in Him,
And be content no matter what state you are in.
Be content and rest in Him in joy and peace,
And only then will your constant longing cease.

Dr. Lydia A. Woods

It's in your contentment, that you'll come to see.
That it's never been about you or me.
That it's only been about the Father and Son,
And becoming a part of the greater One.

And you'll discover all the wealth and riches there,
That are far bigger than any worry or care.
You'll understand that this is not your home.
You'll begin to grow-up and be full grown,

In the realm of the Spirit,
Now you have come up higher,
All frustrations and fears are gone,
And in the Spirit you'll never tire!

Dr. Lydia A. Woods

If You Loved Me Lord...

Romans 8:26; James 4:3 (KJV)

I prayed for riches to give to the poor,
I've proved I'm a giver, so Lord, bless me with more.

I asked, but I didn't get, so what's-up with that,
If You loved me Lord, you'd give – Ain't that a fact!

I prayed continuously for a mate,
It seemed like a good thing for my sake.

I asked, but I didn't get, so what's-up with that,
If You loved me Lord, you'd give – Ain't that a fact!

My prayers never cease for my family to be saved,
But I wonder if they will, before I go to my grave.

I asked, but I didn't get, so what's-up with that,
If You loved me Lord, you'd give – Ain't that a fact!

My prayers go up daily for my poverty to end,
Pressed down, running over, you said, I'd be given to by men.

I asked, but I didn't get, so what's-up with that,
If You loved me Lord, you'd give – Ain't that a fact!

My prayers are never ending for my sickness to cease.
The Word promises me healing and rest in God's peace.

I asked, but I didn't get - so what's-up with that?
If you loved me Lord you'd give ... Ain't that a fact!

Lord I've asked for understanding, speak to me,
I can't hear your voice, I'm blind and can't see.

Acceptance with Joy

I asked, but I didn't get - so what's-up with that,
If you loved me Lord you'd give … Ain't that a fact!

So what am I doing wrong, that I need to quit,
Is it just that I'm whining, and throwing a fit!

Other Christians are praying and getting blessed,
But my praying is fruitless - my life seems a mess.

I've asked other saints about the truth of Your Word,
And their responses to me seem trite and absurd.

They tell me to repent and ask forgiveness for my sin,
That I'm full of pride, my prayers are blowing in the wind.

They say that when I ask, I ask amiss,
I thought it would be easy – So what's up with this?

They say I need to remember that there is a price,
I should be doing my part, it doesn't count just being nice.

I should forgive others, and repent of my sin,
And recognize that it's by faith, the Father's pleasure, I win.

And obedience is important better than sacrifice,
Getting my will in line and daily laying down my life.

Christians that are doers of the Word,
And have a relationship with Christ – Never crack!

I asked, but I didn't get, so what's-up with that,
If You loved me Lord you'd give – Ain't that a fact!

Dr. Lydia A. Woods

It's Alright

James 1:5 (KJV)

I'm like the kid who pesters their mother,
And my father and sisters and even my brother.
Wanting answers to every mysterious wonder,
So many questions – I like to ponder.

I want to know how a tree grows so high?
How many stars are in the sky?
How does a hummingbird really fly?
Mother, mother, please tell me why?

And with the Lord I am just the same,
I pray and pray and call His name.
Wanting answers to problems, clear vision and sight,
But all He says, sometimes is, "It's Alright."

And when I get the "It's Alright," response, it's quite profound,
There is something inside me that settles down.
A peace that floods my very being,
I know the problem is solved without my seeing.

I'm coming to know the Father well,
And about Him to everyone I tell,
About His answers as we talk – that's quite,
Soothing to my Spirit each time I hear, "It's Alright."

Acceptance with Joy

Just Wait!

Psalm 27:14, 25:3, 37:18; Isaiah 40:31 (KJV)

I'm tired Lord, I've had enough,
How many times must I learn this lesson of trust.
I learned to trust you when I had that trial,
I was praising Your Name all the while.

Didn't you see the way I handled myself,
I relied on You and trusted in Your wealth.
I lifted my hands and praised your name,
I worked the Word and drove Satan to shame.

So now that I learned that lesson you see,
I'm ready to move on – now go on and bless me!
Bless me with the riches and desires of my heart,
For Your Word promises me prosperity if I've done my part.

But Saints remember it's not you who decides,
When the lesson is learned and when you have arrived.
It's the Father who knows just when you are ready,
It takes many years to learn to trust and be steady.

Steady and sure, immovable and steadfast,
Waiting on the Lord till you think you can't last.
And just when you think you can't go on,
You'll mount like an eagle and be airborne.

He'll give you strength to continue this race,
Because of His love and mercy and grace.
Be still, shut-up, it's not too late,
Learn to rest in Him and – Just Wait!

Food for Saints   *A Compilation of Christian Poetry*

Dr. Lydia A. Woods

Know Your Enemy

Matthew 4:1-11; Mark 16:17 (KJV)

Come on soldiers, gather round,
We're going to war today on the battleground.

You know the enemy is not very smart,
But he is effective and good at his part.

Let's take the time to get some wisdom here,
My first lesson to you is – never fear!

If you've got the basics about the Father and Son,
Never forget that the battle is already won.

But we must play it out for scripture to be fulfilled,
Take it home to the ending, that will really thrill.

All the Saints and Angelic forces in heaven and earth,
I'm talking about a plan that was forged before your birth.

But it's very important for all Saints to know,
That the enemy is real and to Spiritual warfare go.

For the enemy's weapons are fear and doubt,
He'll try to make you forget what you are all about.

Acceptance with Joy

He'll try to get you to focus the war on your brother,
You'll forget you're commanded to love one another.

He'll make you fearful for your very life,
But remember, you've laid it down, bought with a price.

He doesn't have any new weapons, the old ones work just fine,
For years he's been successful, kicking Saints in the behind.

Satan's plan is simple, it was the same yesterday,
To get you to believe in what he has to say.

Now he continually talks inside your head,
Picking at your weakness and the fears you dread.

The moment you begin to agree with him,
You have sold your birthright and your future is dim.

You've given him power and he can rule,
Over you – so don't be no fool.

Neutralize his weapons ignorance, doubt, confusion and fear,
By using the Name of Jesus on the battlefield frontier!

Dr. Lydia A. Woods

Lean Not

Proverbs 3:5-6; James 1:5 (KJV)

Lean not to thy own understanding,
For you haven't got all the facts.
Take it from the One who knows all,
For your understanding is feeble and lacks.

It lacks, the wisdom of the ages,
It lacks, because you're not full grown.
It lacks, because your wisdom is fuzzy.
It lacks, because of sin that is sown.

I know you made good grades in school.
You've always been told that you are smart.
But your intellect is no good in this realm,
In the Spirit it's faith that sets you apart.

So take your understanding from the Father,
He is wise and has your best interest at heart,
He knows that you are a child just stumbling,
He is willing to pick you up and take your part.

So lean not to thy own understanding,
Ask for wisdom, He will give it freely to you.
For His thoughts and His ways are much higher,
But it's His understanding that will see you through!

Love is an Action

Philippians 4:19 (KJV)

The Child asked the Mother, "Mommy, do you love me?
You didn't tell me today, where is your love, I just don't see."

My darling child, I told you a hundred times today,
Did you not hear me? - I said, I love you in every way.

I told you, I loved you by waking you up,
In preparing your meals and filling your cup.

In providing the roof, over your head,
By turning on the heat, as you slept in your bed.

By driving you to school, giving lunch money and a kiss,
By giving you a hug, whenever you insist.

In combing your hair, and washing your clothes,
And listening to your tales, of junior high woes.

Helping with your homework, and watching the game that you won,
By telling you no ...till your chores are all done.

For my darling, love isn't just words that you say,
Love is an action that you show every day!

So if you are wondering if God really loves you,
Look at your life and see if it's true.

For you are His darling child, He said, "I love you, today,"
'Cause "Love is An Action" that He shows every day!

Dr. Lydia A. Woods

So What's-Up With That!

Malachi 3:13-17 (KJV)

Lord, I don't think, Your Word is true,
Because You haven't done what I asked You to.

It's hard for me to believe, what You say,
Because I see no evidence of Your love today.

Your Word said, "To ask and I would receive,"
If I pray and truly in my heart believe.

But that didn't happen, so What's-Up with that!
This Christian, faith thing, seems a bunch of crap!

Lord, don't you know what I have done,
I've forgiven my brothers and sisters, one by one.

I gave to the poor, when I had none,
Blessed my enemies, everyone.

I've sacrificed and been through many trials,
Believing in You all the while.

So What's-Up With this – cause when I knock,
The door doesn't open, it's bolted tight and locked.

Acceptance with Joy

I feel like I'm beating my head against a stone wall,
I've cried out in my pain, but You don't hear my call.

You said, to seek and I would find,
But all I get is kicked in my behind.

I cannot see Your love for me,
The sinners seem to be living high and free.

They are not calling on Your name from day to day,
They don't even try to practice what You say.

They're winning the lottery and getting dreams fulfilled,
It looks like I'm going backwards or standing still.

I seemed better off before I knew Your name,
I'm feeling most times that I'm going insane.

So what's-up with Your Word, prove something to me,
Give me a sign of Your love so I can see.

Cause if I had a sign you see,
I could believe in Your love for me! – (Not!)

Dr. Lydia A. Woods

Take Out the Trash!

Ephesians 6:18; James 5:13; I Thessalonians 5:17; Romans 8:16 (KJV)

The pressure of living on the earth,
Builds to a fever pitch and you wonder if it's worth,
All the hassle and strain, we all need relief,
We need to take it all to the Lord, that's my belief.

For only He can handle all the stress,
Keep us sane under the pressure of all this mess,
Sometimes we forget to give it all to Him, we are remiss,
One day He explained it to me just like this.

How often do you take out your trash,
That's filled with leftovers like corned beef hash,
Rotten tomatoes, meat, and potato peels,
Paper, and bottles – this situation is real!

It's serious business if the trash isn't taken out,
You'd have a serious problem without a doubt.
Do you really want me to describe the mess there would be,
The smell would be out of this world – you see!

Well in the Spirit a process like this exists,
The Spirit fills with trash, now I must insist.
That you "work" with me here as I explain,
This parable that the Lord has put in my brain.

Acceptance with Joy

We must dump that garbage from our spirits, 'cause I suspect
It's been building quite some time because of your neglect.
To take the garbage out in a consistent way,
Now admit that you've not been taking it out every day.

You may take out that little trash every now and then,
But the big stuff's been building that – unrepented sin.
Now when I finally can't stand that funky smell in me,
It's to the throne room, I'm running to the arms of thee!

Now the scene is not pretty, these sessions with Him,
Standard equipment is a towel and repentance from sin.
I cry and cry as the Holy Spirit reveals to me my sin,
And shows me the denial that I have been in.

That feeling of God's forgiveness overwhelms and comforts me,
I wipe my tears and now I'm able to see.
That the rotten garbage has now been released,
Revelation begins to flood me and my pain begins to cease.

I have a new walk and a deeper faith when it is done,
"So take out the Trash," often – Give it all to His Son!

Dr. Lydia A. Woods

Unable to Receive

Luke 6:38; Malachi 3:10 (KJV)

He will pour out a blessing of which you can't conceive.
So big and mighty you can't even receive.

Have you ever had that feeling of "can't even receive,"
You get choked up and can't speak, the tears won't recede.

The blessing is shaken together, running over and pressed down.
There isn't a cup big enough to be found.

That can contain His blessing and love for you,
So just hold on and be blessed – What else can you do?

Dr. Lydia A. Woods

With Persecution...

Matthew 5:10-12; II Corinthians 4:9-18 (KJV)

Now when you dine at the Lord's table,
He's serving up a meal, fit for a king.
But you better know what's served with redemption,
It's a dish called – "*With Persecution.*"

Now of all the dishes served by the Lord,
"*With Persecution,*" is a bitter dish indeed,
And none of His children take pleasure or delight,
In that dish that is served most every night.

The Father insists that – "*With Persecution,*" be served,
That no meal is quite ever complete without,
But His children all moan and groan and pout,
For they question this dish without a doubt.

Why add – "*With Persecution,*" to every meal,
What ingredients are so special inside,
The taste is so darn unpleasant,
Will it grow our hair or make one wise?

Acceptance with Joy

The Father knows that – "*With Persecution*,"
Builds strong Spiritual bones,
Helps our digestion of long-suffering and humble pie,
And after just a little while,
You'll just come to accept it and not question why.

Then slowly you'll begin to understand,
That "*With Persecution*," is a necessary dish indeed,
That the making of mature Saints is the purpose,
And "*With Persecution*," helps every Saint to succeed,

In our growing process here on earth,
As we come to understand the purpose of our birth,
Just pass that dish down this way,
I'm going to enjoy me some – "*With Persecution*," Today!

Let Those With Ears...

Dr. Lydia A. Woods

Answer to Many a Prayer

John 16:33; Romans 5:3, 12:12 (KJV)

Trials and tribulations are the answer,
To many a prayer,
You probably don't want to believe this,
But I truly swear,

That in many cases this really,
Is absolutely true,
You know in your heart,
That I'm being straight with you.

Don't pray to take,
The trials and tribulations away,
The old folk say, pray for strength,
To endure them day by day.

Those trials and tribulations are tools,
Used to shape and mold,
For He who began a good work,
Finishes, it I am told.

The potter molds the clay,
With tribulations and trials,
Knowing it can be painful,
For just a little while.

Acceptance with Joy

Think of trials and tribulations,
As the potters hands,
They love and caress you,
As He accomplishes His plans.

In many of those prayers you ask,
For great wisdom and knowledge,
Not the kind you get,
From attending a fancy college.

You ask – Lord make me,
Loving, and ever so kind,
Make me a giver, a good steward,
Lord give me Your mind!

I want gentleness and understanding,
And discipline for sure,
And the most sought after of all,
Is faith to endure.

Well, all of these prayers,
Can be answered just so,
Trials and tribulations my dears,
Takes care of them all – Didn't You Know!

Dr. Lydia A. Woods

Blood Disguise

Ephesians 1:7; Acts 20:28; Hebrews 9:22 (KJV)

Imagine God looking down,
From Heaven and on His face a frown.

Because He is only able to look,
Upon that which has no sin -- It's in the book!

So how does He look upon me?
So full of sin, I know His eyes will not see,

The very person who I want to be,
Holy, pure, righteous and sin free.

"Don't worry," He said, to me,
I've provided a way so you – I can see,

Just cover yourself in my Son's blood,
Which unites us together in perfect love.

For the Blood of My Son covers sin,
And now my children are able to come in.

To the presence of My Holy eyes,
Under this precious Blood Disguise!

Dr. Lydia A. Woods

Boys Into Men

Isaiah 54:13; Hebrews 12:6; Revelation 3:19 (KJV)

In the name of Love, parents can commit great sin,
Doing good to their children, that's when trouble begins!

With that misguided love, of helping them out,
You can ruin a good child, without a doubt.

Even though our Father can give us all we desire,
He withholds it, to save us from hell's fire.

So when I became a single parent, to three young men,
I'll share this conversation, I had with the Lord then.

Lord only You know how to make, boys into men,
I'm turning them over to You, so please begin.

He spoke to my heart and said, this to me,
"You must stay out of My way, wait on Me and see."

For what I'm about to do, will turn you inside out,
But I'll make men of your boys, never have a doubt.

Through the years He has reminded me, of how we began,
Me trusting in His knowledge, of how to make a man.

He knows just how to mold, that boy into a man,
He knows how to shape a girl, into a woman with His hand

Acceptance with Joy

Now here is the secret, be sharp or you will miss,
The wisdom in these next lines, will surely assist.

First and last – parents get out of the Lord's way,
'Cause it's painful to see your child suffer, even a little today.

But remember that the suffering, will strengthen that back,
God won't kill or maim them, that's a guaranteed fact!

Don't give that money, even though you have plenty,
Don't let them move back in, even if there's room for many.

Don't buy that car, or loan that money -- Not today!
Don't pay for that college, or credit card – No way!

You'll look like the bad guy, you surely can bet.
But suck it in – be tough – 'cause you'll never regret.

You didn't create a monster, that turns on you with its hate,
You didn't handicap your son or daughter, before it was too late.

That you allowed the Lord, to make your, boy into a man,
And that girl into a woman, able to on her own stand.

You'll be proud one day, of the fine job the Lord did,
That He made a Man or Woman, out of your precious Kid!

Dr. Lydia A. Woods

The Building You Call Church

Colossians 1:18; Matthew 16:18; Ephesians 5:27 (KJV)

It's Sunday morning and I'm going to church!
How impossible a thought this is to me.

The church is not a building,
It's not a place to go.
The church is people,
Saints, I know – You know.

The Church is the bride of our Lord,
He loves her with His life,
The Church is preparing herself,
Spot and wrinkle free to be His holy wife.

You are the building not made with hands,
A place for the Spirit of God to dwell,
It's very important to get this right,
And of course, saints, you know, I'm going to tell.

Because if you see yourself as God sees you,
Engaged to be a wife to His Son,
A temple fit to hold His precious Spirit,
You'll begin to see that God's victory is won.

Don't assign your birthright to a building,
That can do no earthly good,
That can't carry the Spirit of the Living God,
To a hurting world as it should.

So get up every morning, not just Sunday,
Let me hear these words, just say,
I'm going to take the Church this morning,
And minister to a hurting world today!

Don't Forsake the Assembly

Hebrews 10:25; Matthew 18:20 (KJV)

To me this is the most abused phrase,
In the Book.
I'm tired of the usage,
Just to get people hooked.

To keep them in bondage,
To keep them coming back,
You know it's your duty,
So don't be slack!

Tell me where it says that,
This phrase really means
On Sunday morning and Wednesday evening,
Every saint should be seen,

Assembling together for the purpose,
Of worship or to edify,
I'm just asking a simple question,
Please tell me why?

My Book says, "where two or three are gathered,"
He will be there.
It never says,
When, how many times or even where.

If I am missing the point,
Please set me straight,
'Cause man's traditions,
Really give me a huge headache!

𝓔.𝓣.

(E.T. – The Movie) John 14:1-4 (KJV)

You've all seen the movie,
But what you didn't see,
Is that E.T. looks,
A lot like you and me.

Now he was left on earth,
By those he loved.
And he searched for their return,
In the heavens above.

I'm sure he volunteered,
To be part of the crew,
To complete the task,
That they came to earth to do.

But the job got a little complex,
And scary towards the end.
He didn't bargain for all the trouble,
That befell him.

Phone home E.T.,
So your people will know,
That you have had enough of earth,
And you are ready to go!

They pursued you and sought,
To take your life,
Why did they leave you here,
With all this strife?

Acceptance with Joy

What lessons have you learned,
In your brief stay,
You met some gentle and loving people,
Along the way.

But what about those others,
Who were full of fear,
Because of your difference,
You became a threat here.

But you left your mark,
And touched some souls,
You showed them love,
The young and the old.

Your purpose completed,
They did come back for you,
And you were changed,
By this earthly experience too.

The spiritual message in that film,
Speaks to you and me,
For this strange place earth,
Is grievous you see,

Lord I identify with E.T.,
And long to be,
Back home with You,
In Eternity!

Dr. Lydia A. Woods

Fruit Trees

Galatians 5:22-23 (KJV)

There's much talk about fruit,
In the Bible, you know.
But not the kind that in a garden,
You can grow.

Can't pick it,
From a plant or bush or tree,
Or find it,
In your neighborhood grocery.

Now there are nine kinds,
Of fruit for your delight,
But you can't see them,
With your natural sight.

And they are planted,
In the oddest place, you know,
In the heart of humans,
Is where this fruit will grow.

For humans are the tree,
So the Word of God tells,
Where all the potential,
For this fruit to grow dwells.

Acceptance with Joy

And you can tell,
If the tree is good,
And if the fruit is growing,
As it should.

Now these nine kinds of fruit,
Let me remind,
Are love, joy and peace,
Just one of a kind.

Also long-suffering, gentleness,
Goodness and faith,
Meekness, and temperance,
All in their place.

They all grow from one tree,
Now that seems strange.
But the heart of a reborn human,
Has been rearranged.

By the Spirit of God,
Who is seed for this amazing tree,
Let these nine precious fruit grow,
In abundance in you and me.

Dr. Lydia A. Woods

Now pass out,
Your fruit every day,
To those you meet,
Along life's way.

Make sure the fruit,
Is fresh and pure,
For the substance of life,
In this fruit will endure,

The evils of this world,
And prevail over the wicked one,
And bring us safely home,
When the job is done!

Generations in You

Psalm 127:3-5, 128:3 (KJV)

I have so many desires and dreams,
This life isn't long enough it seems.

For me to fulfill all that I want to do,
It's frustrating for me to attempt to.

But the Lord explained it to me just so,
So that I wouldn't get too anxious, you know.

That in all my dreams and desires,
Is just the vision of generations inspired.

The deeds of my children, grandchildren and more,
Lay in me, for I am just a door.

To the future of all that God has planned,
To accomplish through me by His loving hand.

So don't regret what you didn't become,
It will happen in a grandchild, or daughter or son.

You didn't sacrifice your life in vain for the kids,
That famous painter, or athlete in future will live.

My soul is at peace,
My footsteps have been ordered by Him,
I look forward to the fulfillment in them.

All my dreams, I will fulfill through my seed,
This is God's amazing fantastic plan indeed!

Dr. Lydia A. Woods

The Gift

Psalm 111:10; Proverbs 16:16-25 (KJV)

Wisdom is the gift,
You want to give away,
But nobody seems to want it,
In this present day.

It's a valuable thing,
You'll pay a precious price,
It costs blood, sweat and tears,
And a piece of your life!

Not money, or silver,
Not even gold,
Can buy this precious thing,
Possessed by the old.

The old one wishes to make a gift,
To the young,
To friends and family,
To daughters and sons.

But no one seems,
To want to take it free,
They all choose to buy their own,
So let them be.

Acceptance with Joy

Let them pay,
With their own blood, sweat, and tears,
For to pay for that thing,
Called wisdom could take years.

So in buying your wisdom,
Buy this too,
That you can't give it to just anyone,
Only those who,

God sends to you,
Now you can give it away.
But hold tight,
To the wisdom until that day.

The giving is usually not to children,
Relatives, or friends
But a stranger who crosses your path,
Every now and then.

And with wisdom you'll begin,
To recognize,
Just who of those strangers,
Will cherish the prize!

Dr. Lydia A. Woods

Has Done, Is Doing or Will Do

Psalm 71:15, 35:28, 40:5; Job 9:10 (KJV)

I have a sister in the Lord,
That lives at a distance from me.
It's a long distance call,
So I use nine cents a minute, 'cause it ain't free.

So we can't call often,
And when we do there's quite a need,
For a Saint who knows the Word,
And has revelation on what they read.

And sometimes that need is just to report,
About what He has done, is doing or will do.
Now here's the thing that struck me the other day,
When the call was done and we were through.

You know a strange thing seems to happen,
I've noticed every time, without fail,
That my feet no longer touch the ground,
And for the time being Satan is back in hell.

Acceptance with Joy

Just to talk about the Lord,
What He has done, is doing or will do,
Delights and thrills His soul,
And He takes pleasure in me and you.

And we are both edified and strengthened,
And ready to face the trials ahead.
Where two or more are gathered in His name,
Is much deeper than at first I read.

There's a blessing to be found,
Just to speak about His Word,
What He has done, is doing or will do,
This is revelation I've never heard.

So keep the conversation about others,
And negative things far from you,
Invest in bragging on the Lord,
What He has done, is doing or will do!

Dr. Lydia A. Woods

Holy Rollers

I Peter 1:23, 2:9; John 1:12-13; I John 5:1 (KJV)

In downtown Chicago,
On street corners you'll see,
Men ranting, repent,
Jesus loves you and me.

Quoting scriptures, dirty clothes,
Unshaven, not clean.
They make you think serving God,
Is a crazy man's thing.

It makes you afraid,
'Cause it's quite extreme.
To be avoided at all cost,
You know what I mean.

Then there are those,
We used to call "Holy Roller" types,
In church all day long,
And into the nights.

Every other word from their mouth,
Is, "Thank You Lord,"
And all they can talk about,
Is the Jesus they adore.

Acceptance with Joy

I never wanted those,
"Holy Rollers" to bother me,
Cause they talked so strange,
I just wanted to flee!

But when I got saved,
A funny thing happened to me,
My eyes were opened,
And I began to see.

My ears could hear,
And I lost the fear,
And any testimony of the Lord,
And His Word I loved to hear.

And I'll talk about Him if you let me,
Night and day,
And I'll talk to anyone interested,
In what I have to say.

Now it has occurred to me,
What the Lord has secretly done.
One of those "Holy Rollers,"
I have without a doubt become!

Dr. Lydia A. Woods

Jesus Learned Obedience

Hebrews 5:8 (KJV)

Obedience is learned –
Not something that happens suddenly,
It isn't automatic,
It's earned, not free.

If you are raising children,
You know what I mean,
Teaching lessons over and over,
Can cause many a scene!

Why don't children just learn,
The first time that we teach,
But they get mad at us,
And say – all we do is preach,

About cleaning their rooms,
And washing the dishes,
They accuse us of never,
Considering their wishes.

And we know their wishes,
Are to play and play,
To eat our food,
And spend our money every day.

Being with their friends,
And having a good time,
Is all that they ever have,
On their minds.

Acceptance with Joy

Their flesh is not designed,
To heed our words about chores.
They think we come from another planet –
Just very big bores!

Their flesh is not designed,
To bow to our will,
Do you ever get this comment,
"Mom or dad – just chill!,"

If you want to understand,
How we treat God?
See the similarities between our children –
It isn't so odd!

Let's face it Saints,
We want to have it our own way,
We don't want to heed,
What the Lord has to say!

He sounds like an alien,
From outer space,
His Words are too hard,
To endure in this place.

Who wants to learn obedience,
It takes too much time.
And this suffering thing,
Are you out of your mind!

Dr. Lydia A. Woods

Take that suffering thing,
Somewhere else,
I'm getting over in this life,
I'm out for myself.

But out for myself,
Is not what it's all about,
That's a short-lived trip,
Without a doubt.

Jesus suffered obedience,
For all mankind,
Boy! He must have been completely,
Out of His mind!

Dr. Lydia A. Woods

Just Give It!

Acts 20:35; Luke 6:34-38 (KJV)

A borrower nor,
A lender be,
Just a giver,
Cause it makes you free.

Free from violating,
Your Father's Word.
And honoring the teaching,
That you have heard.

There's bondage in borrowing,
From a friend.
Or a neighbor or bank,
And especially your kin.

Have you noticed that things tend,
To get in the way,
Trying to make it impossible,
For that debt to pay.

And when you are the lender,
Things are going on there,
Cause you're expecting your money back,
Just your fair share.

They said they would pay,
And you took it for true,
Now they can't be found –
Are they avoiding you?

Acceptance with Joy

Now resentment for that person,
Is building in your heart,
Because there was good and pure,
Intentions on your part.

Now there is a mess,
Between friends or your kin,
And both of you have fallen,
So easily into sin,

They had every intention,
Of paying it back,
Why does it always happen,
That they get sidetracked?

Now that's the wisdom,
In the Word you see,
And these kinds of problems,
Need never be.

Me mad at you,
And you resenting me,
Just give it!
Honor the Word, and be Free!

Dr. Lydia A. Woods

Liar, Liar

II Timothy 2:11; Romans 6:3-4 (KJV)

Liar, Liar,
Pants on fire,
Can't pee as high,
As a telephone wire!

You remember this one,
From back in the day,
When you and your friends,
Were outside at play.

Remember the whoppers,
You told back then,
Your were only being creative,
It wasn't a sin.

But put away those childish things,
Now my dear,
I call you to truth,
Be honest and sincere.

When you say that you've given,
Your life to Christ,
Engaged to the bridegroom,
And hope to be His wife.

Acceptance with Joy

Now be careful here 'cause this,
Is the important part,
Remember you can't keep even a small piece.
Of your heart.

Every body part, thought,
Deed and desire,
Everything in life,
That you have acquired.

The day you gave,
Your heart to Him,
It was only about two percent of you,
My friend!

That gets you in the game,
Now you're ready to play,
I'm telling you the truth,
About your salvation day!

The Lord wants every bit and part,
All of you,
But even you can't give you,
Like you want to,

Dr. Lydia A. Woods

Cause you're not suicidal,
And you love your life,
You're not giving it up,
Without a fight.

And a fight is what you're going to get,
In this new walk,
Do a couple of rounds with Satan,
Then let's hear you talk.

You start giving,
That life up bit by bit,
There are many times,
You think to quit.

But you know you can only go,
Forward from here,
So you strive to be closer to the One,
You love so dear.

The One who can,
Cut a raw diamond to clear perfection,
The Father who gives us,
Much loving, needed correction.

The One who helps the baby grow,
Into a woman or man.
The potter who molds and remolds,
With His skilful hands.

Acceptance with Joy

The One who breaks the wild horse,
So it's fit to ride,
The One who will never ever,
Leave your side.

So don't be,
In denial today,
Just keep giving Him your life,
In every way.

And don't be ignorant,
Of what He has begun,
He's out for all of you,
And He'll not lose even one!

Dr. Lydia A. Woods

My God Isn't Stupid!

Genesis 2:8-9 (KJV)

Concrete cities designed to kill,
Destroy gardens, trees, and mountainous hills.

Man thrives in a garden you know,
So to kill him place him where nothing will grow.

There is no life in concrete and stone.
Definitely no place for flesh and bone.

Tiny living spaces stacked very high,
Crowded together and do you know why?

A master plan to destroy the seed,
Who is capable of this dreadful deed?

The wicked one destroys, kills, and steals,
It's a simple plan and Satan is for real.

Look how man has fallen for this evil plan.
Destroying the earth and water, forest and land.

Hunting animals to extinction, polluting the air,
It could make one worry or even despair.

But there is a time appointed by the Holy One,
We must always remember,
That the victory is already won.

In this latter day it looks like we'll all regret,
But like I always say, My God isn't Stupid!

Acceptance with Joy

Not in a Place Called Church

II Peter 2:1-3; II Timothy 2:15; II Corinthians 6:16 (KJV)

Saints, I'll not have you ignorant.

Of the many voices,
And teachings in the world today,
It's big business to say "I've come in His name,"
And lead many a flock astray.

For their doctrines are filled with vanity and proof,
Clouding your mind and the Word's very truth.
If you are not schooled in the Word you'll believe,
That a preacher is gifted and you'll follow their lead.

You must study to show yourself approved and equipped,
To judge what you hear so you will not slip,
Into following the many voices in the air,
And every wind of doctrine – Please, Saints beware.

Precious Saints never follow any man's lead.
For the Word is within and that's all you need.
Don't get caught worshipping the creature.
For Jesus sent the Comforter as your only teacher.

You won't find Him in a place called "Church," not today!
But in a place not made with hands the scriptures say.
That place lies within the human heart,
Now isn't that one of our many body parts?

Know ye not that your body is the temple in this day,
Go there to seek the Lord and hear Him say,
All that you need to know and understand,
About your purpose and how to live as He commands.

Dr. Lydia A. Woods

Obedience the Highest Form of Praise

Hebrews 5:8; Romans 5:19; Philippians 2:8 (KJV)

Raise your hands in the congregation,
And call it praise!

Pray in many glorious words,
And call it praise!

Sing in your most beautiful voice,
And call it praise!

Dress in your finest apparel,
And call it Praise!

Play loudly on fine instruments,
And call it Praise!

Build the finest buildings,
And call it Praise!

Meet often with the Saints,
And call it Praise!

Work in your churches,
And call it Praise!

Obedience is the highest form, of Praise I know.
Obedience is frankly, the only route to go.
What is this obedience, that she is talking about?
Make it clear to me, without a doubt!

Acceptance with Joy

Jesus learned obedience, by the things that He suffered.
Now what are these things, that are used for buffers?
Things that make you want, to run away in fear.
Things that are not pleasing, to your flesh, my dears.

Things that don't make sense, to your mind.
Things that literally kick you, in the behind.
Things that you know, he told only to you.
Things that are against what family, wants you to do.

Things that will cause you, grief and pain.
Things that will make you feel, a little deranged.
Things that you won't run out, and do right away.
Things that take time and suffering before you'll say.

Lord, I will gladly do it, because I've conquered the fear,
And finally I see clearly, my purpose here.
I must voluntarily lose my life to gain it, for that is your plan.
This sometimes takes a lifetime, to understand.

My life and my will I'll fight, to the death to keep.
But it's to the death, that I freely give it to God, so I can reap.
The greatest reward, that obedience can possibly win,
Is to reign with His Son in eternity – Free from Sin!

Dr. Lydia A. Woods

The Perfect Murder

Romans 7:14-21 (KJV)

The perfect murder, I plot at night,
My enemy to put permanently out of sight!

It has ruined my life, so it must go,
I'm talking about my *Will* – you know.

I've tried to kill it many times before,
I've kicked it to the curb and out the door.

It won't stay dead or get in line.
But maybe it *Will* stay dead this time!

'Cause this time, I'm giving it up to the One,
Whose dealt with *Will* since times begun.

Since killing it is not the way,
I'll give it to God each and every day.

It's not killing that He has in mind,
But little adjustments made over time.

He's slowly lining it up with His own will,
'Cause a *Will* is something you just can't kill!

Dr. Lydia A. Woods

Resistance is Futile

I Corinthians 6:17, 12:12-27 (KJV)

Resistance is futile,
Trekkies know just what I mean.
The Borg is coming,
And it's a hopeless, frightening thing.

Wherever they go,
The purpose is clear.
To assimilate – and resistance,
Is futile, my dear.

Well that was Hollywood's version,
Of the way it ought to be,
But if you understand the plot,
I know you will see.

That the Borg's plan isn't original,
They took their cue,
From the master planner,
Who is assimilating me and you.

Acceptance with Joy

Now if you resist – you remember,
The consequence of the Borg,
Either assimilate or be destroyed,
The choice is all yours.

Individual entities,
With one collective mind,
Working for an evil purpose,
To destroy all life forms and humankind.

Now the collective mind of God,
Is just the opposite you see,
To give eternal life to humankind,
And to set them forever free.

Free from evil, death and sin –
Please assimilate me now!
I will not put up a fight,
Because Resistance is Futile!

Dr. Lydia A. Woods

So Great a Cloud of Witnesses

Hebrews 12:1 (KJV)

Now that great cloud of witnesses,
Is watching as you run.
This race that's set before you,
Filled with hazards and hurdles,
Not quite my idea of fun.

I got a mental picture,
As I talked with a Saint the other day,
Of the size and number of the hurdles,
That we encounter along the way.

I was describing my life,
In racing terms of course,
I had just taken a big hurdle,
Caught my foot and hit the turf.

Now I'm lying on the track.
Scraped knees, bleeding hands, wounded pride,
And I look to the left,
As runners pass me right in stride.

I lay there for a moment,
Waiting for assistance from on High,
I'm moaning and groaning nursing my wounds,
And feeling like I might as well just die.

Acceptance with Joy

But death is not in the picture,
'Cause that's the easy way out.
I'm expected to pick myself up,
Take joy in my affliction, without doubt,

That I'm going to make it to the end,
Of this lifelong race that's set out for me.
Running hurdles in the dark,
With only faith to carry me.

But besides the faith to finish,
Just remember the league you're in,
For that Great Cloud of Witnesses,
Is cheering for your success to win.

And I heard that Cloud of Witnesses,
Just the other day.
As I pulled myself up from another fall,
And was stewing in my dismay.

That Cloud of Witnesses was great.
The number I couldn't quite make out.
And they were cheering rather loudly,
As if I was winning without a doubt.

Dr. Lydia A. Woods

I realized at that moment,
That it didn't matter the shape I was in,
'Cause this race is not about strong or swift,
But enduring to the end.

Endurance isn't pretty,
Cause every mark has a tale to tell.
Of the battles with Satan,
In the very depths of hell.

But it's about the race,
And the cleansing process along the way.
So that we can stand without spot or blemish,
In His presence on that Day!

Dr. Lydia A. Woods

The U.P.S. Man

John 4:44; Psalm 105:15 (KJV)

Do you get mad at the UPS man
When he delivers your package into your hands?

If you don't like what's delivered to you,
Notify the sender that's what you do.

Now that's all a prophet does you see,
Delivers messages from God to you and me.

But a prophet is not liked in their own land,
Cause being prophetic is not in high demand.

It's not easy being a prophet, speaking what God has to say,
To a rebellious people, not so different than back in the day.

If the news is good, please tell me more,
But keep bad news to yourself, or just hit the door.

So just treat a prophet like the UPS guy,
Thank them kindly, close the door, cause this is why,

The UPS man didn't send that package to you,
If you have a problem with it, You know Who to take it to!

Upside Down, Inside Out

Romans 1:21-32 (KJV)

Make no mistake about it,
We're living in the time of the end.
Everything is upside down and inside out,
It doesn't seem like we can win.

Don't feel sorry for the victim,
'Cause the crook's a battered child.
Violence all around us,
Homosexuality right in style.

Compassion seems nonexistent,
Keep hustling to get ahead.
The pressure is tremendous,
Folk's jumping from bed to bed.

Killing babies, hurting children,
Homelessness and hunger in your face.
Rapidly heading for destruction,
Will there be no winners in this race?

The race is not given to the swift or the strong,
But time is running out, where is the end?
Upside down and Inside out,
Lord Jesus, deliver us from this world of sin!

Dr. Lydia A. Woods

With His Own Blood

Acts 20:28; Hosea 2:19; Revelation 19:7-9, 21:9 (KJV)

I love a love story,
As most women do.
Give me a happy ending,
Plus boxes of tissue too.

I'll cry you a bucket,
In the dark of any show.
'Cause a love story pulls,
At my heartstrings, anyway it goes.

Well the greatest love story ever written,
I know of in this life,
Is the love of Jesus Christ for the church,
His sought after wife.

The most romantic thing I know,
Is a man laying down His life,
For the woman that He loves,
For His precious, beloved wife.

The horrible death that He suffered,
So that His beloved could only live.
Is the most beautiful gift of love,
That anyone can give.

My favorite hymn ever,
I've loved it since a child.
The melody sweetly haunts me,
As I hum the tune awhile.

Acceptance with Joy

"From heaven He came and sought her,
To be His holy bride,
With His own blood He bought her,
And for her life He died.*"

But not like Romeo and Juliet,
Star-crossed lovers in that tale,
That only in death,
Can they together dwell.

Our love story is unsurpassed,
For not even death can hold,
This lover in the grave,
That's how this love story goes.

The ending tells,
Of the greatest victory won,
For God so loved the world,
He gave His only Son.

After giving up His life,
For His beloved precious Bride,
He is raised again to life,
And awaits her by His Side!

---

* "The Church's One Foundation" By Samuel J. Stone and Samuel S. Wesley

Conversations with the Saints

Dr. Lydia A. Woods

Ain't He All That!

Hebrews 1:2-3; John 1:1-5; Revelation 22:13 (KJV)

You've heard the young people say…
That he or she "Ain't all that,"
I know One whose "All That" and that's a fact.

Ain't He All That – and then some.
He's Alpha and Omega the Holy One.

Ain't He All That – and that's for sure,
Sent for the Salvation of man – earth's cure.

Ain't He All That – and you know why?
Cause He's the only One that can satisfy.

Ain't He All That – just look around you and attest,
He's head and heels over all the rest.

Ain't He All That – He can take away pain,
Heal broken hearts, save sinners with no strain.

Ain't He All That – a place to safely run,
In times of trouble, He's the only One.

Ain't He All That – for the care and love,
He's all that – Our Father above!

- Conversation with Ms. Elizabeth J. Jackson

Dr. Lydia A. Woods

A Blessing – Not a Curse!

Psalm 127:3-5 (KJV)

It is written, children are a Blessing not a curse,
But a bunch of kids – What could be worse?

They suck your time and money, kill your dreams,
It's a long hard haul, and so it seems.

That for the present I wonder how and why,
These kids will bless me by and by.

To sacrifice your life's blood - And children just take,
At times it seems having them was a big mistake.

If you've walked that path you know what I mean,
Especially, if you have survived the teens!

Each stage brings joys, frustrations and fears,
Will they ever mature -- These little dears?

But if you ask me if I'd do it all again,
Without a doubt I would answer, yes, my friend.

Acceptance with Joy

Cause when I beheld my new precious grandson,
I knew deep joy and gladness had really begun.

I never realized that the next step would be,
Generations through my seed for me to see,

A strange feeling of happiness in God's plan,
To bring generations through the seed of man,

Being a door to life, is worth all the pain,
The plan is quite amazing and simple to explain.

That a bunch of kids - What could be worse?
Children are a blessing -- Not a curse!

— Conversation with Mr. Gene Wideman

Dr. Lydia A. Woods

Call My Name

I Peter 2:9 (KJV)

The Lord allows you to put some living under your belt,
Before He calls your name and His urging is felt.

He first set His love on you – not the other way round,
So don't think it's your idea – when the Lord you have found.

He calls you out of darkness into His marvelous light,
In the Lamb's Book of Life your name He writes.

But you can't accept Him as your Lord, until that day,
You must wait on the Lord, before you can say.

"Lord come into my life, change me, save me, please,"
So until that time, you are just one of these.

One of the lost sheep, waiting to be found,
But the shepherd hasn't forgotten, soon you'll be kingdom bound.

He'll leave the ninety-nine on your behalf,
And you'll soon be guided by His rod and staff,

The Angels will rejoice and many Saints too,
The moment you take Him for your own and say – I do.

Until your name is called many Saints water and plant,
But God gives the increase, so I repeat – You can't!

Just take the Lord any time as your Savior to proclaim,
You must wait your turn, until – He Calls Your Name!

- Conversation with Ms. Delores Johnson

Acceptance with Joy

Cerebral Palsy

Philippians 1:6; I Thessalonians 5:24; I Corinthians 1:9 (KJV)

For a parable of the present day Church, I'll need,
To borrow Cerebral Palsy, as an example, please.

The brain sends signals for the body to heed,
But the limbs don't follow the brain's careful lead.

One leg goes sideways when it should go straight,
One arm goes left or right when it should wait,

The head it jerks, the trunk is not quite right,
Every body part is trying with all its might.

To follow the directions coming from the head,
But something is wrong there is confusion instead.

Where there is confusion, every work of Satan can be found,
The Body of Christ looks to the world like a foolish clown.

Seems to me this interference must be moved out of the way,
For the Church to function perfectly as it should, today.

Jesus is our hope and He's coming you can bet,
And that interference will be put in a lake that is not wet!

- Conversation with Ms. Gloria Roe

Dr. Lydia A. Woods

Common Sense

I Corinthians 1:25, 3:19; II Corinthians 5:7; Proverbs 3:5-6 (KJV)

"You know God gave us, "common sense,"
People say this every day,
But it's not common sense we need,
But faith in God, to help us find our way,

Make no mistake about the world,
With its rules and hatred for God's Word,
Trying to figure it out with your head,
Is a fruitless venture – I have heard.

For the Word says the foolishness of God,
Will confound the wisdom of man,
His ways and thoughts are not ours,
We need faith and the Holy Spirit to understand.

For without faith as your sixth sense,
You will perish in your sin,
Using "common sense" and reason,
In this earth realm you can never win.

Lean not to thy own understanding,
That is "common sense" to me,
Don't rely on the "common sense," of this world,
That will never lead to life or eternity.

- Conversation with Ms. Gloria Roe

Dr. Lydia A. Woods

Convicted

Romans 7:14-25 (KJV)

Satan is good at what he does - make no mistake,
Setting up Saints to partake, of his evil bait.

After the first bite of his delicious cake,
You curse your very life - your flesh you hate.

I'd been walking with the Lord so very long,
I didn't believe I could do, this kind of wrong,

I know the Word, so very well,
How could I do this thing, from the pit of hell?

You immediately feel sick, you know what I mean,
The pleasure you thought you'd have from doing the thing,

Only leaves' you broken, feeling you have betrayed,
Your heavenly Father – it's the saddest of days.

You want to turn the clock back, just a little bit,
Repeat the decision, 'cause you have been tricked.

Fallen for the trap, of the evil one,
Lord forgive the weakness, in your daughters and sons.

But the Lord has made provision, 'cause he knows us well,
In His Son, who has the keys to the Kingdom and hell.

Acceptance with Joy

It is written,
"Repent and turn away from your sin,"
He'll forgive you and salvation is yours, in the end.

Yes, He will forgive you, but you have a price to pay,
Forgiving yourself often gets in your way.

It's hard to move past, that sin you've committed,
But one day in your testimony, you'll gladly admit it.

That you fell that time, but the Lord was good,
It made you a better person, and you understood,

That what was meant for evil, God turned to your good,
And His purpose was accomplished, as it should.

But the conviction of the Holy Spirit – we all will feel,
'Cause the Father loves His children, and that's for real!

He chastises those He calls His own, and that is why,
You should take comfort at this time, that you Qualify!

— Conversation with Mr. Vestell C. Royal

Dr. Lydia A. Woods

Denominations

Mark 3:24-25; I Corinthians 12:12-31 (KJV)

Denominations whose brilliant plan is this?
It's surely not God's – I must insist.

It has the markings of you-know-who,
Cause it divides Christians – me against you.

Now how crazy it all seems to me,
Serving the same God, but we can't agree!

You interpret the Word this way not that,
We differ on almost every single fact.

Our denomination has all the truth, over here,
And our group is going in – not yours, my dear.

A house divided on itself shall surely fall,
Jesus taught this in His Word to one and all.

I look forward to the day when denominations cease,
And the Body of Christ works for God's purpose in peace.

Serving one God must include one single plan,
And in this plan denominations cannot ultimately stand.

The enemy is good at trying to destroy,
By dividing us with this denominational ploy.

Lord, we wait patiently, searching the heavens above,
Looking for that perfect ending of unity in love.

- Conversation with Mr. William C. Terry

Forgive or Forgive Not

Luke 6:37; Mark 11:25-26 (KJV)

Forgive or forgive not, the choice is up to you.
But choose wisely and carefully, whatever you do!

For to forgive not - can seal your very fate,
By eating you alive, with a cancer of consuming hate.

But to forgive - now you're talking my language here,
The sweetest of gestures, frees your Spirit, my dears!

Dr. Lydia A. Woods

He's Good At...

Genesis 1:3, 9, 12, 16, 24, 27, 31; Isaiah 14:27, 46:9-11 (KJV)

He's good – you've got to give it to Him,
Didn't need help creating angels, man or cherubim,

He's good – 'cause He made all that you see,
Canyons, flowers, bugs, rivers and the mighty tree.

He's good at – making the sun,
The moon, skies and stars every one,

He's good at – making mountains and lakes,
He's just good for goodness sake,

He's good at – making women and men,
And loving them in spite of their constant sin,

He's good at – accomplishing His own plan,
Through the lives of any woman, child, or man.

He's good at – what He does,
That's why we are here and He's above.

He's good at – solving our little messes,
That He turns into our greatest successes.

He's good at – blessing us too,
I'm trying to figure how -- He do what He do!

He's good at – and He is -- All that!
So just accept that -- He's Good At!

- Conversation with Ms. Delores Johnson

Dr. Lydia A. Woods

If Thou Be...

Matthew 4:6 (KJV)

If thou be the Son of God,
Satan's question to Jesus -- Now that was odd!

Satan knew He was the only begotten Son,
Was he just fooling around, having a bit of fun?

Is Satan so stupid or something worse,
To expect Jesus to serve him and His Father curse?

Jesus came to do the Father's Will,
And Satan knew it -- so what's the deal?

Now I've always thought Satan, not to bright,
To question Jesus on the issue of His birthright,

And if he would question Jesus with so stupid a plan,
Then he'll put the question to any ordinary woman or man.

Yes, Satan questions our birthright day in and out,
Trying to cause confusion and set up doubt.

Acceptance with Joy

And his stupid plan has worked like a charm,
Saints are giving him power and being disarmed.

Questioning their birthright has caused many to doubt,
They have power to foil his plan and wipe him out.

Power given to them through the Holy Name,
Step up with faith and your birthright claim.

So that whosoever that believes in Him,
Can through faith in Jesus their Salvation win.

And when Satan questions -- If Thou Be ...
Say, It is Written -- and there is no doubt in me!

- Conversation with Ms. Serena Reese

Dr. Lydia A. Woods

If You Will Be Great

Matthew 20:26; I Peter 5:3 (KJV)

If you will be great, a servant you'll be,
That's what Jesus told the disciples – trust me.

The feet of them Jesus washed to make it clear,
That to be great in the kingdom – be a servant, my dear.

Now down here on earth, who plays the servant's part,
The job of a mother qualifies – she has a servant's heart.

She is the door of life into the earth, for the seed,
And she catches it most from the enemy, indeed.

She ministers to the least of these – you know,
The children in her care, she nurtures to grow.

In the end times many mothers have emerged strong,
Have taken the challenge to become Spiritually full grown.

Satan has attacked the family, and it's down on its knees,
But Jesus has the victory and He has the keys.

And a mere servant girl can beat the enemy to shame,
'Cause she has access to the keys and Jesus' precious name.

So mothers step up and receive your servant's pay,
You have a place of Honor in the Kingdom, Today!

- Conversation with Ms. Elizabeth J. Jackson

Dr. Lydia A. Woods

Just a Family Feud

Genesis 12:2, 17:6, 18:18 (KJV)

I was discussing with a Saint, about our Family Tree,
How big and flourishing, it must now surely be.

The family of humankind was our immediate concern,
The Holy Spirit came on board to help us learn.

We started from the beginning, just talking and mapping it so,
I wanted a huge wall to draw on to see how big it would grow.

There was Adam and Eve, Noah and his three sons,
Ham, Japheth and Shem, three great nations had begun.

Through Shem's line came our father Abraham with great faith,
With Ishmael and Isaac, two important nations in their place.

And of course through Isaac the Promise manifested,
Our Lord and Savior Jesus Christ was begot and then tested.

He was found pure, a proper unblemished Lamb, God's man,
Then sacrificed to redeem us all as part of the glorious plan.

Acceptance with Joy

The gentiles given a chance to become children by faith,
Those born of Abraham's seed, also redeemed by grace.

It's "Just a Family Feud," and who do you think is winning?
Well, I can tell you this, one day it will all stop – This sinning!

We must remember, family members, are noted for their love,
One to another, which pleases their heavenly Father above.

We are all of one family serving the One True God,
No matter what you call Him – now isn't that odd.

That we should all be fighting for an inheritance and a place,
In God's Holy presence - One day we'll all stand face to face.

Brothers and sisters of every kindred and race,
Each in His kingdom by our Father's Mercy and Grace.

                    - Conversation with Mr. William C. Terry

Dr. Lydia A. Woods

The Kingdom is Like Unto...

Matthew 4:23, 13:10-11, 13:31-33, 20:1-16, 24:14, 25:1-30 (KJV)

"The Kingdom is Like Unto," is what Jesus proclaimed,
And they that heard His words would never be the same.

He testified of a place He knew that was glorious and fine.
So different from anything people had heard at that time.

Over and over examples of the Kingdom and its glory,
Why so many references, story after story?

It must have been very important for us to know,
For to the multitudes He taught them just so.

He taught them in parables, and the disciples inquired,
The meanings in private and He granted their desire.

He explained to the disciples that those with ears,
Would understand and take hope from their fears.

He told the disciples that they should take heed,
And understand the parable of the "Sower and the Seed,"

Acceptance with Joy

For in this one, all parables they could understand,
That they were blessed above many a righteous man.

The prophets and righteous men desired to see those things,
That Jesus taught and the freedom – Kingdom brings.

So why aren't we following Jesus' lead today?
Teaching in parables and on the Kingdom way,

The Kingdom is like unto… – It was good enough back then,
Making citizens of the Kingdom of women and men.

Jesus has come into His Kingdom it's here on earth,
Through every man, woman and child in the new birth.

If we practice Kingdom living in this earth, we'll live to tell,
How we overthrew Satan and stormed the gates of hell.

- Inspired By
Hannah Hunnard - Thank you for your precious books!

Dr. Lydia A. Woods

Love You - Not Your Sin

Romans 1:26-27 (KJV)

Just recently in the news the other day,
A discussion of what the Church had to say.

Gay and lesbian lifestyles all the rage,
But God's Word warns us on almost every page,

In the latter days humans will disregard what I say,
Heap to themselves teachers in the modern day.

Those who interpret to please their own mind,
Justifying their sin, leaving righteousness behind.

Now come on Church let's get back to the basics,
Let not sin rule us today in the Holy places.

That Holy place, where God resides is the temple,
It's not too difficult, but really quite simple.

Acceptance with Joy

The temple where I reside is within you,
So put away the sin you were born to.

Set aside your sin, do not fulfill the lust,
For to reign with Me you - Just must!

Each of us are born into sin,
Some sin more obvious to condemn,

Each of us struggling to live holy and pure,
And to bear our cross, overcome and endure.

Never the person should the Church condemn,
For God loves us -- but not our sin.

- Conversation with Mr. Gene Wideman

Dr. Lydia A. Woods

Only Human!

II Corinthians 5:17, 6:16 (KJV)

People will say, "You know you're only human."
Justifying the mistakes they make,
But if you are born again as I am,
I'm a "new creature" for heaven's sake.

I get a little irritated,
It gets under my skin for sure,
I no longer see myself as human,
But a creature full of power, holy and pure.

With what is dwelling on the inside of me,
I no longer qualify for the human race,
I've been elevated above the earth,
No longer functioning in time and space.

For the Spirit realm is my home,
I wage war on the enemies of God,
He has prepared me for such a fight,
We are a peculiar people, strange and odd.

This "New Creature" has wondrous power,
Over Satan and all spiritual beings from hell,
I just want to scream, we're no longer human,
I want to run and to everyone tell.

Acceptance with Joy

This new creature has been commanded to go,
Into all of the world and proclaim,
That the kingdom is come here on earth,
Through Jesus Christ we will never be the same.

Jesus has all power and the keys,
To heaven and earth and hell's gates,
So accept the Spirit let it come in,
A new creature is what it's gonna take,

To live in this world no ordinary humans,
To stand, and then stand, in that evil day,
Take hold of God's awesome mighty plan,
Which provides for His victory in this way.

He will dwell in these Holy temples,
In the last days, not made with hands,
Creating New Creatures in Jesus Christ,
Out of plain ordinary Humans!

Dr. Lydia A. Woods

Pro-Choice?

Mark 3:4; Exodus 20:13 (KJV)

You had "Pro-Choice" without a doubt,
But now you don't want to stick it out.

You laid right down and did that thing,
Knowing full well what that action might bring.

Your "Pro-choice" created a precious human life,
But now it's causing too much worldly strife.

Now your "Pro-choice" is this life to take,
'Cause you want the "Pro-choice" to separate.

It's my body and I don't want to share,
But of this sin you must beware.

Now to both – that body of yours is needed,
Both with rights to life unimpeded.

The law of man must protect each side,
So I'm afraid for nine months you must abide.

"Pro-Choice" you had it at first to make,
Your second "Pro-choice" we can't allow you to take!

- Conversation with Mr. Gene Wideman

Dr. Lydia A. Woods

Puzzling

Genesis 1:26 (KJV)

I've always enjoyed a good puzzle, you know,
The whole family round the table, enjoying it so.

Especially, round the holidays when it's very cold,
Off to the store for a puzzle, so my story goes.

Now the five hundred pieces we finish in a night,
The one thousand pieces, now that's a challenging sight.

A couple of day's work but we knock it out just fine,
Fitting pieces together – Stimulating our minds.

Each working in their little corner or space,
Grabbing at pieces sometimes it seems like a race.

I like looking for that little splash of yellow or red,
On the corner of her hat or the cover on the bed.

I like seeing it all somehow take form and shape,
Matching the picture on the box – Oh! I love to create!

A few more puzzles we finished this past holiday,
But it got me to thinking about the Lord's way.

I notice that life is like a giant puzzle you see,
God revealing the pieces of our lives – Now here's the key!

Acceptance with Joy

Suddenly, a piece is revealed clear to view,
It's fitted, then you see what was forming in you.

Now that only completes just a corner or section of you,
But I'm, always surprised 'cause I hadn't a clue.

Now a little more of the plan for your life is revealed,
One day the puzzle will be finished which once was concealed.

So now I understand that – I am the puzzle – There is a plan,
Scattered pieces being formed by the master's own hand.

He's working to complete my puzzle – Hurry please!
I'm trying to be patient, but I just want to see.

What will the likeness of my puzzle finally be,
Look child, it's the image of God – That I see!

- Conversation with Mr. Jeffrey Proctor and
Ms. Maria Kwiatkowski

Dr. Lydia A. Woods

Sabbath Day

Exodus 20:8-11; Luke 6:5 (KJV)

I recently had Saints ask me in seriousness,
Which day is Sabbath? Could you please address?

Is Sabbath Saturday or Sunday, can you tell me please?
I want to be in God's will – I want to appease!

I want to keep God's commandments in every way,
So could you please tell just which one is the day?

My response is one somewhat hard to understand,
For "Sabbath" is not a day – An explanation you demand?

For you have always been taught it was a "day,"
Let me explain it to you, just this way.

There are rituals and symbols in the Bible that conceal,
Hidden truths that are now to His Saints being revealed.

The hidden truths of "Sabbath" was revealed to me,
Now through the Holy Spirit, I want you to see.

Acceptance with Joy

"Sabbath" represents His precious Son, now can't you guess?
Created for man to relieve his labors on earth for perfect rest.

"Sabbath" was made for man, not the other way round.
Jesus is "Lord of the Sabbath," this is quite profound.

Jesus said, "come unto me ye who labor indeed,"
Your burden is heavy and in this world you will need,

One such as Me, who can give you relief,
From the labors of this world, I want you to cease.

He doesn't just want you to rest, in Him on only one day,
But every day in Jesus is God's perfect created way.

God sanctified and hallowed this precious day,
And only Jesus can be Holy and Sanctified in this way.

A "day" cannot be Holy, only the Christ – you'll realize,
So take this revelation knowledge and in this grow wise.

Be released from bondage to serving and esteeming a day,
And through Jesus our "Sabbath" know a more excellent way.

- Conversation with Mr. William C. Terry

Dr. Lydia A. Woods

Seeds of Self-Destruction

James 1:26, 3:5-10; Proverbs 18:21, 25:23 (KJV)

Seeds of self-destruction, planted when we're young,
The tender, innocent child, unaware that it's begun.

If the seeds of self-destruction take root and have their way,
Satan's plan will be accomplished in us today!

Parents, relatives, and friends are the willing ones,
They do Satan's bidding with their wagging foolish tongues.

Instead of building you up, they speak about your lack,
Your precious sensitive feelings get trampled, just like that!

The cruelty of those words, the acts of unkind deeds,
They all contribute to the growing of self-destruction seeds.

By the time you become adult, the seed has blossomed into a tree,
And there is ugly hideous fruit, growing in you and me.

The seeds are various kinds - I'll name them for you,
There is self-doubt, self-hatred, self-frustration now you have a clue.

They produce low self-esteem, lack of confidence, and the like,
Changing our appearance to fit some standard to be right.

Acceptance with Joy

A standard that is self-destructive it denies just who you are,
You look into the mirror - you've turned into something quite bizarre!

If the seeds of self-destruction, go according to the plan,
Then Satan only has to wait for the destruction of man,

But God has a plan too, that calls you into His marvelous light,
A slow process begins that will put you back to right.

For what Satan meant for evil to destroy, steal and kill,
We have a powerful weapon of defense – the human will.

And when we will to serve the Lord, we become new on the inside,
Those seeds of self-destruction can no longer in us abide.

The wicked plan has been overthrown; he is losing as I speak,
It sounded like a good one, but it was faulty and quite weak.

For no plan of self-destruction that Satan could ever think of,
Can stand against the forces of God's profound and precious love!

— Conversation with William C. Terry

Dr. Lydia A. Woods

Take No Thought

Luke 12:22-30 (KJV)

Take no thought – For what you should wear,
Take no thought – In this world of cares.

Take no thought – For your Father will provide.
If you'll only let Him – He will satisfy.

Take no thought – For where you should live.
Only learn that in any state you find yourself—Give!

Take no thought – For what you should eat,
For the Lord will supply your food, drink and meat.

Take no thought – For any need,
For He is faithful to fulfill this promise indeed.

Take no thought – I know it's easy to say,
But if you will practice, it's the only way,

Take no thought – Means to renew that mind,
Every day to achieve perfection divine.

Take no thought – Is the ultimate tribute indeed,
For without *Faith* it's impossible to please.

Take no thought – Is the only way to live down here,
Free from worry, disappointment, frustration and fear.

Take no thought, I'll say no more,
Just leave it all to the One we Adore!

There But For the Grace...

Luke 10:27-37; Matthew 22:39 (KJV)

There but for the Grace of God - Go I,
These words I've often wondered why?

How can the murderer, prostitute, drunk be me!
Look deeper friend and you will see.

There but for the Grace - Go you or I,
And so you ask the question ... Why?

That same question asked to the Master long ago,
Who is my neighbor? - Explain it so...

That I may know just who they are,
Are they near or are they far.

Love your neighbor as yourself, the great command,
My neighbor *is* myself, now I understand.

The inner being created just like me,
No differences that I can see!

I could be them - But for the Grace,
I see myself within every face.

I look into the souls of men,
I see myself reflected within,

So you are me and I am you,
From one God, one source, one family grew.

Compassion swells, I now know why,
There but for the Grace of God - Go I.

- Conversation with Mr. Gene Wideman

Dr. Lydia A. Woods

Tower of Babel

Genesis 11:1-10 (KJV)

The whole earth was of one same tongue,
And all could understand each and every one.

The people planned to make themselves a name,
To build a city and tower, to their own acclaim.

The Lord came down to see what they had done,
The city and tower they had begun.

He knew that being together and of one mind,
There was nothing to restrain – This humankind.

He confounded their speech – confusion set in,
Their evil plans went into a downward tailspin.

There is a lesson to be learned – So Church take heed,
One accord, one language is important for us to succeed.

Where there is division and confusion every work exists,
Of the enemy and his purpose to accomplish.

Denominations are just another "Tower of Babel," from old,
It scatters and divides us from accomplishing our goal.

Let's take heed from the Word that leads and guides,
To all wisdom and truth and in one mind abide.

- Conversation with Ms. Elizabeth J. Jackson

Dr. Lydia A. Woods

True Way of Life

John 13:34-35, 14:6 (KJV)

One day the Lord said to me,
When you think of Jesus what do you see?

I said, there is an image of a man in my mind,
Strong, gentle in spirit, loving and kind.

Then God said something that astonished me,
I'll forever change what you see.

He is not a man but something much more,
My Word will reveal what you missed before.

I am the Truth, the way and the life, He said.
Ponder this a moment inside your head.

Now say it all together, God said to me
I am a true way of life – Now what do you see?

Not a man, but a plan – A concept big and vast,
This answers some of my questions at last.

I was blown away –
My understanding was opened that day.
I wanted to hear more of what the Lord had to say.

Acceptance with Joy

He opened my understanding the light was bright in my head,
It was hard to take in all that He said.

If Jesus is a true way of life, then this means,
There is only One Way to enter that door it seems.

That "True Way of Life" is simple to understand,
Love God with your whole self and your fellow man.

Then you have lived that true life indeed,
And there is evidence that you are His seed.

Then one can enter through the door if the life is pure,
Because you truly know Jesus and that's for sure.

It's not about what a mouth will say,
It's about the evidence in your life from day to day.

I am the Truth, the Way and the Life – Live it and see,
Your life will tell if you really knew Me!

— Conversation with Bill, Keith, and Rick

Dr. Lydia A. Woods

What's Your Problem?

Mark 16:15-18 (KJV)

If you have ever heard this man do his thing,
I'm talking about a precious Saint named, David Ring!

He gives a testimony that will surely inspire,
I listen to his tapes and never tire.

He was born the youngest in a family of seven,
A preacher's kid - a blessing from heaven.

He was born with cerebral palsy and his body was affected,
He suffered many things, was taunted and rejected.

His father went to be with the Lord – Oh how he cried,
And his sorrow was complete when his beloved mother died.

He wanted to die; his heart was broken and torn,
He lamented the day that he was born.

His sister was the only one, who didn't give up on him,
Like a good sister she nagged through thick and thin.

Acceptance with Joy

To get her off his back he went to church that day,
And Jesus changed his life in a mighty way.

The Lord healed his heart and called him to preach,
With his shaking body and jumbled speech.

Now he's preaching the Word of the gospel of Christ,
He's married with kids and a beautiful wife.

He reminds us all; who are healthy and strong,
That if he can work for the Kingdom - Then what is wrong?

My favorite part of his testimony is this,
As he convicts us all who would resist,

The call that the Lord has on each life, Your excuse can't stand,
"What's your problem healthy woman, healthy man!"

- Inspired by Mr. David Ring

Scriptural References

Poems by Revelation

Dr. Lydia A. Woods

A Bible Character

Luke 22:47, 57, 60; 23:21-34; Mark 15:1, 10-11, 16:1;
Matthew 21:24; I Peter 2:9 (KJV)

Luke 22:47 (KJV)
47 And while he yet spake, behold a multitude, and he that was called Judas, one of the twelve, went before them, and drew near unto Jesus to kiss him.

Luke 22:57 (KJV)
57 And he denied him, saying, Woman, I know him not.

Luke 22:60 (KJV)
60 And Peter said, Man, I know not what thou sayest. And immediately, while he yet spake, the cock crew.

Luke 23:21-34 (KJV)
21 But they cried, saying, Crucify him, crucify him.
22 And he said unto them the third time, Why, what evil hath he done? I have found no cause of death in him: I will therefore chastise him, and let him go.
23 And they were instant with loud voices, requiring that he might be crucified. And the voices of them and of the chief priests prevailed.
24 And Pilate gave sentence that it should be as they required.
25 And he released unto them him that for sedition and murder was cast into prison, whom they had desired; but he delivered Jesus to their will.
26 And as they led him away, they laid hold upon one Simon, a Cyrenian, coming out of the country, and on him they laid the cross, that he might bear it after Jesus.
27 And there followed him a great company of people, and of women, which also bewailed and lamented him.
28 But Jesus turning unto them said, Daughters of Jerusalem, weep not for me, but weep for yourselves, and for your children.

Acceptance with Joy

29 For, behold, the days are coming, in the which they shall say, Blessed are the barren, and the wombs that never bare, and the paps which never gave suck.
30 Then shall they begin to say to the mountains, Fall on us; and to the hills, Cover us.
31 For if they do these things in a green tree, what shall be done in the dry?
32 And there were also two other, malefactors, led with him to be put to death.
33 And when they were come to the place, which is called Calvary, there they crucified him, and the malefactors, one on the right hand, and the other on the left.
34 Then said Jesus, Father, forgive them; for they know not what they do. And they parted his raiment, and cast lots.

Mark 15:1 (KJV)
1 And straightway in the morning the chief priests held a consultation with the elders and scribes and the whole council, and bound Jesus, and carried him away, and delivered him to Pilate.

Mark 15:10-11 (KJV)
10 For he knew that the chief priests had delivered him for envy.
11 But the chief priests moved the people, that he should rather release Barabbas unto them.

Mark 16:1 (KJV)
1 And when the sabbath was past, Mary Magdalene, and Mary the mother of James, and Salome, had bought sweet spices, that they might come and anoint him.

Matthew 21:24 (KJV)
24 And Jesus answered and said unto them, I also will ask you one thing, which if ye tell me, I in like wise will tell you by what authority I do these things.

I Peter 2:9 (KJV)
9 But ye are a chosen generation, a royal priesthood, an holy nation, a peculiar people; that ye should shew forth the praises of him who hath called you out of darkness into his marvellous light;

Birthright

Genesis 27:1-46; 28:1-22 (KJV)

Genesis 27:1-46 (KJV)
1 And it came to pass, that when Isaac was old, and his eyes were dim, so that he could not see, he called Esau his eldest son, and said unto him, My son: and he said unto him, Behold, here am I.
2 And he said, Behold now, I am old, I know not the day of my death:
3 Now therefore take, I pray thee, thy weapons, thy quiver and thy bow, and go out to the field, and take me some venison;
4 And make me savoury meat, such as I love, and bring it to me, that I may eat; that my soul may bless thee before I die.
5 And Rebekah heard when Isaac spake to Esau his son. And Esau went to the field to hunt for venison, and to bring it.
6 And Rebekah spake unto Jacob her son, saying, Behold, I heard thy father speak unto Esau thy brother, saying,
7 Bring me venison, and make me savoury meat, that I may eat, and bless thee before the LORD before my death.
8 Now therefore, my son, obey my voice according to that which I command thee.
9 Go now to the flock, and fetch me from thence two good kids of the goats; and I will make them savoury meat for thy father, such as he loveth:
10 And thou shalt bring it to thy father, that he may eat, and that he may bless thee before his death.
11 And Jacob said to Rebekah his mother, Behold, Esau my brother is a hairy man, and I am a smooth man:
12 My father peradventure will feel me, and I shall seem to him as a deceiver; and I shall bring a curse upon me, and not a blessing.
13 And his mother said unto him, Upon me be thy curse, my son: only obey my voice, and go fetch me them.

¹⁴ And he went, and fetched, and brought them to his mother: and his mother made savoury meat, such as his father loved.
¹⁵ And Rebekah took goodly raiment of her eldest son Esau, which were with her in the house, and put them upon Jacob her younger son:
¹⁶ And she put the skins of the kids of the goats upon his hands, and upon the smooth of his neck:
¹⁷ And she gave the savoury meat and the bread, which she had prepared, into the hand of her son Jacob.
¹⁸ And he came unto his father, and said, My father: and he said, Here am I; who art thou, my son?
¹⁹ And Jacob said unto his father, I am Esau thy first born; I have done according as thou badest me: arise, I pray thee, sit and eat of my venison, that thy soul may bless me.
²⁰ And Isaac said unto his son, How is it that thou hast found it so quickly, my son? And he said, Because the LORD thy God brought it to me.
²¹ And Isaac said unto Jacob, Come near, I pray thee, that I may feel thee, my son, whether thou be my very son Esau or not.
²² And Jacob went near unto Isaac his father; and he felt him, and said, The voice is Jacob's voice, but the hands are the hands of Esau.
²³ And he discerned him not, because his hands were hairy, as his brother Esau's hands: so he blessed him.
²⁴ And he said, Art thou my very son Esau? And he said, I am.
²⁵ And he said, Bring it near to me, and I will eat of my son's venison, that my soul may bless thee. And he brought it near to him, and he did eat: and he brought him wine and he drank.

Acceptance with Joy

26 And his father Isaac said unto him, Come near now, and kiss me, my son.
27 And he came near, and kissed him: and he smelled the smell of his raiment, and blessed him, and said, See, the smell of my son is as the smell of a field which the LORD hath blessed:
28 Therefore God give thee of the dew of heaven, and the fatness of the earth, and plenty of corn and wine:
29 Let people serve thee, and nations bow down to thee: be lord over thy brethren, and let thy mother's sons bow down to thee: cursed be every one that curseth thee, and blessed be he that blesseth thee.
30 And it came to pass, as soon as Isaac had made an end of blessing Jacob, and Jacob was yet scarce gone out from the presence of Isaac his father, that Esau his brother came in from his hunting.
31 And he also had made savoury meat, and brought it unto his father, and said unto his father, Let my father arise, and eat of his son's venison, that thy soul may bless me.
32 And Isaac his father said unto him, Who art thou? And he said, I am thy son, thy firstborn Esau.
33 And Isaac trembled very exceedingly, and said, Who? where is he that hath taken venison, and brought it me, and I have eaten of all before thou camest, and have blessed him? yea, and he shall be blessed.
34 And when Esau heard the words of his father, he cried with a great and exceeding bitter cry, and said unto his father, Bless me, even me also, O my father.
35 And he said, Thy brother came with subtilty, and hath taken away thy blessing.

³⁶ And he said, Is not he rightly named Jacob? for he hath supplanted me these two times: he took away my birthright; and, behold, now he hath taken away my blessing. And he said, Hast thou not reserved a blessing for me?
³⁷ And Isaac answered and said unto Esau, Behold, I have made him thy lord, and all his brethren have I given to him for servants; and with corn and wine have I sustained him: and what shall I do now unto thee, my son?
³⁸ And Esau said unto his father, Hast thou but one blessing, my father? bless me, even me also, O my father. And Esau lifted up his voice, and wept.
³⁹ And Isaac his father answered and said unto him, Behold, thy dwelling shall be the fatness of the earth, and of the dew of heaven from above;
⁴⁰ And by thy sword shalt thou live, and shalt serve thy brother; and it shall come to pass when thou shalt have the dominion, that thou shalt break his yoke from off thy neck.
⁴¹ And Esau hated Jacob because of the blessing wherewith his father blessed him: and Esau said in his heart, The days of mourning for my father are at hand; then will I slay my brother Jacob.
⁴² And these words of Esau her elder son were told to Rebekah: and she sent and called Jacob her younger son, and said unto him, Behold, thy brother Esau, as touching thee, doth comfort himself, purposing to kill thee.
⁴³ Now therefore, my son, obey my voice; arise, flee thou to Laban my brother to Haran;
⁴⁴ And tarry with him a few days, until thy brother's fury turn away;

⁴⁵ Until thy brother's anger turn away from thee, and he forget that which thou hast done to him: then I will send, and fetch thee from thence: why should I be deprived also of you both in one day?
⁴⁶ And Rebekah said to Isaac, I am weary of my life because of the daughters of Heth: if Jacob take a wife of the daughters of Heth, such as these which are of the daughters of the land, what good shall my life do me?

Genesis 28:1-22 (KJV)
¹ And Isaac called Jacob, and blessed him, and charged him, and said unto him, Thou shalt not take a wife of the daughters of Canaan.
² Arise, go to Padanaram, to the house of Bethuel thy mother's father; and take thee a wife from thence of the daughers of Laban thy mother's brother.
³ And God Almighty bless thee, and make thee fruitful, and multiply thee, that thou mayest be a multitude of people;
⁴ And give thee the blessing of Abraham, to thee, and to thy seed with thee; that thou mayest inherit the land wherein thou art a stranger, which God gave unto Abraham.
⁵ And Isaac sent away Jacob: and he went to Padanaram unto Laban, son of Bethuel the Syrian, the brother of Rebekah, Jacob's and Esau's mother.
⁶ When Esau saw that Isaac had blessed Jacob, and sent him away to Padanaram, to take him a wife from thence; and that as he blessed him he gave him a charge, saying, Thou shalt not take a wife of the daughers of Canaan;
⁷ And that Jacob obeyed his father and his mother, and was gone to Padanaram;

⁸ And Esau seeing that the daughters of Canaan pleased not Isaac his father;
⁹ Then went Esau unto Ishmael, and took unto the wives which he had Mahalath the daughter of Ishmael Abraham's son, the sister of Nebajoth, to be his wife.
¹⁰ And Jacob went out from Beersheba, and went toward Haran.
¹¹ And he lighted upon a certain place, and tarried there all night, because the sun was set; and he took of the stones of that place, and put them for his pillows, and lay down in that place to sleep.
¹² And he dreamed, and behold a ladder set up on the earth, and the top of it reached to heaven: and behold the angels of God ascending and descending on it.
¹³ And, behold, the LORD stood above it, and said, I am the LORD God of Abraham thy father, and the God of Isaac: the land whereon thou liest, to thee will I give it, and to thy seed;
¹⁴ And thy seed shall be as the dust of the earth, and thou shalt spread abroad to the west, and to the east, and to the north, and to the south: and in thee and in thy seed shall all the families of the earth be blessed.
¹⁵ And, behold, I am with thee, and will keep thee in all places whither thou goest, and will bring thee again into this land; for I will not leave thee, until I have done that which I have spoken to thee of.
¹⁶ And Jacob awaked out of his sleep, and he said, Surely the LORD is in this place; and I knew it not.
¹⁷ And he was afraid, and said, How dreadful is this place! this is none other but the house of God, and this is the gate of heaven.

Acceptance with Joy

¹⁸ And Jacob rose up early in the morning, and took the stone that he had put for his pillows, and set it up for a pillar, and poured oil upon the top of it.
¹⁹ And he called the name of that place Bethel: but the name of that city was called Luz at the first.
²⁰ And Jacob vowed a vow, saying, If God will be with me, and will keep me in this way that I go, and will give me bread to eat, and raiment to put on,
²¹ So that I come again to my father's house in peace; then shall the LORD be my God:
²² And this stone, which I have set for a pillar, shall be God's house: and of all that thou shalt give me I will surely give the tenth unto thee.

Dr. Lydia A. Woods

Bringing His Family Out

Genesis 3:22-24; Mark 1:14-15; I Peter 2:9; I Corinthians 2:12; Ephesians 1:3-6; Acts 2:17; Matthew 24:21-22; Hebrews 10:38 (KJV)

Genesis 3:22-24 (KJV)
22 And the LORD God said, Behold, the man is become as one of us, to know good and evil: and now, lest he put forth his hand, and take also of the tree of life, and eat, and live for ever:
23 Therefore the LORD God sent him forth from the garden of Eden, to till the ground from whence he was taken.
24 So he drove out the man; and he placed at the east of the garden of Eden Cherubims, and a flaming sword which turned every way, to keep the way of the tree of life.

Mark 1:14-15 (KJV)
14 Now after that John was put in prison, Jesus came into Galilee, preaching the gospel of the kingdom of God,
15 And saying, The time is fulfilled, and the kingdom of God is at hand: repent ye, and believe the gospel.

I Peter 2:9 (KJV)
9 But ye are a chosen generation, a royal priesthood, an holy nation, a peculiar people; that ye should shew forth the praises of him who hath called you out of darkness into his marvellous light;

I Corinthians 2:12 (KJV)
12 Now we have received, not the spirit of the world, but the spirit which is of God; that we might know the things that are freely given to us of God.

Ephesians 1:3-6 (KJV)
3 Blessed be the God and Father of our Lord Jesus Christ, who hath blessed us with all spiritual blessings in heavenly places in Christ:

Acceptance with Joy

[4] According as he hath chosen us in him before the foundation of the world, that we should be holy and without blame before him in love:
[5] Having predestinated us unto the adoption of children by Jesus Christ to himself, according to the good pleasure of his will,
[6] To the praise of the glory of his grace, wherein he hath made us accepted in the beloved.

Acts 2:17 (KJV)
[17] And it shall come to pass in the last days, saith God, I will pour out of my Spirit upon all flesh: and your sons and your daughters shall prophesy, and your young men shall see visions, and your old men shall dream dreams:

Matthew 24:21-22 (KJV)
[21] For then shall be great tribulation, such as was not since the beginning of the world to this time, no, nor ever shall be.
[22] And except those days should be shortened, there should no flesh be saved: but for the elect's sake those days shall be shortened.

Hebrews 10:38 (KJV)
[38] Now the just shall live by faith: but if any man draw back, my soul shall have no pleasure in him.

Dr. Lydia A. Woods

The Day of His Birth

Genesis 1:26-27; Luke 2:6-14 (KJV)

Genesis 1:26-27 (KJV)
26 And God said, Let us make man in our image, after our likeness: and let them have dominion over the fish of the sea, and over the fowl of the air, and over the cattle, and over all the earth, and over every creeping thing that creepeth upon the earth.
27 So God created man in his own image, in the image of God created he him; male and female created he them.

Luke 2:6-14 (KJV)
6 And so it was, that, while they were there, the days were accomplished that she should be delivered.
7 And she brought forth her firstborn son, and wrapped him in swaddling clothes, and laid him in a manger; because there was no room for them in the inn.
8 And there were in the same country shepherds abiding in the field, keeping watch over their flock by night.
9 And, lo, the angel of the Lord came upon them, and the glory of the Lord shone round about them: and they were sore afraid.
10 And the angel said unto them, Fear not: for, behold, I bring you good tidings of great joy, which shall be to all people.
11 For unto you is born this day in the city of David a Saviour, which is Christ the Lord.
12 And this shall be a sign unto you; Ye shall find the babe wrapped in swaddling clothes, lying in a manger.
13 And suddenly there was with the angel a multitude of the heavenly host praising God, and saying,
14 Glory to God in the highest, and on earth peace, good will toward men.

Acceptance with Joy

Doin' the Israelite

Exodus 11:2, 13:21, 14:27-28, 16:2-3,12, 17:2-4 (KJV)

Exodus 11:2 (KJV)
2 Speak now in the ears of the people, and let every man borrow of his neighbour, and every woman of her neighbour, jewels of silver and jewels of gold.

Exodus 13:21 (KJV)
21 And the LORD went before them by day in a pillar of a cloud, to lead them the way; and by night in a pillar of fire, to give them light; to go by day and night:

Exodus 14:27-28 (KJV)
27 And Moses stretched forth his hand over the sea, and the sea returned to his strength when the morning appeared; and the Egyptians fled against it; and the LORD overthrew the Egyptians in the midst of the sea.
28 And the waters returned, and covered the chariots, and the horsemen, and all the host of Pharaoh that came into the sea after them; there remained not so much as one of them.

Exodus 16:2-3 (KJV)
2 And the whole congregation of the children of Israel murmured against Moses and Aaron in the wilderness:
3 And the children of Israel said unto them, Would to God we had died by the hand of the LORD in the land of Egypt, when we sat by the flesh pots, and when we did eat bread to the full; for ye have brought us forth into this wilderness, to kill this whole assembly with hunger.

Exodus 16:12 (KJV)
12 I have heard the murmurings of the children of Israel: speak unto them, saying, At even ye shall eat flesh, and in the morning ye shall be filled with bread; and ye shall know that I am the LORD your God.

Exodus 17:2-4 (KJV)
² Wherefore the people did chide with Moses, and said, Give us water that we may drink. And Moses said unto them, Why chide ye with me? wherefore do ye tempt the LORD?
³ And the people thirsted there for water; and the people murmured against Moses, and said, Wherefore is this that thou hast brought us up out of Egypt, to kill us and our children and our cattle with thirst?
⁴ And Moses cried unto the LORD, saying, What shall I do unto this people? they be almost ready to stone me.

Get a Testimony

Luke 4:18-19; James 1:2-4 (KJV)

Luke 4:18-19 (KJV)
18 The Spirit of the Lord is upon me, because he hath anointed me to preach the gospel to the poor; he hath sent me to heal the brokenhearted, to preach deliverance to the captives, and recovering of sight to the blind, to set at liberty them that are bruised,
19 To preach the acceptable year of the Lord.

James 1:2-4 (KJV)
2 My brethren, count it all joy when ye fall into divers temptations;
3 Knowing this, that the trying of your faith worketh patience.
4 But let patience have her perfect work, that ye may be perfect and entire, wanting nothing.

Getting to Know You

Proverbs 1:7, 2:1,3:1-4 (KJV)

Proverbs 1:7 (KJV)
7 The fear of the LORD is the beginning of knowledge: but fools despise wisdom and instruction.

Proverbs 2:1 (KJV)
1 My son, if thou wilt receive my words, and hide my commandments with thee;

Proverbs 3:1-4 (KJV)
1 My son, forget not my law; but let thine heart keep my commandments:
2 For length of days, and long life, and peace, shall they add to thee.
3 Let not mercy and truth forsake thee: bind them about thy neck; write them upon the table of thine heart:
4 So shalt thou find favour and good understanding in the sight of God and man.

Good News

I Corinthians 15:3, 15:52; Mark 13:24-27; Revelation 1:7, 19:7-9, 20:1-3, 21:1-5 (KJV)

I Corinthians 15:3 (KJV)
3 For I delivered unto you first of all that which I also received, how that Christ died for our sins according to the scriptures;

I Corinthians 15:52 (KJV)
52 In a moment, in the twinkling of an eye, at the last trump: for the trumpet shall sound, and the dead shall be raised incorruptible, and we shall be changed.

Mark 13:24-27 (KJV)
24 But in those days, after that tribulation, the sun shall be darkened, and the moon shall not give her light,
25 And the stars of heaven shall fall, and the powers that are in heaven shall be shaken.
26 And then shall they see the Son of man coming in the clouds with great power and glory.
27 And then shall he send his angels, and shall gather together his elect from the four winds, from the uttermost part of the earth to the uttermost part of heaven.

Revelation 1:7 (KJV)
7 Behold, he cometh with clouds; and every eye shall see him, and they also which pierced him: and all kindreds of the earth shall wail because of him. Even so, Amen.

Revelation 19:7-9 (KJV)
7 Let us be glad and rejoice, and give honour to him: for the marriage of the Lamb is come, and his wife hath made herself ready.
8 And to her was granted that she should be arrayed in fine linen, clean and white: for the fine linen is the righteousness of saints.

⁹ And he saith unto me, Write, Blessed are they which are called unto the marriage supper of the Lamb. And he saith unto me, These are the true sayings of God.

Revelation 20:1-3 (KJV)
¹ And I saw an angel come down from heaven, having the key of the bottomless pit and a great chain in his hand.
² And he laid hold on the dragon, that old serpent, which is the Devil, and Satan, and bound him a thousand years,
³ And cast him into the bottomless pit, and shut him up, and set a seal upon him, that he should deceive the nations no more, till the thousand years should be fulfilled: and after that he must be loosed a little season.

Revelation 21:1-5 (KJV)
¹ And I saw a new heaven and a new earth: for the first heaven and the first earth were passed away; and there was no more sea.
² And I John saw the holy city, new Jerusalem, coming down from God out of heaven, prepared as a bride adorned for her husband.
³ And I heard a great voice out of heaven saying, Behold, the tabernacle of God is with men, and he will dwell with them, and they shall be his people, and God himself shall be with them, and be their God.
⁴ And God shall wipe away all tears from their eyes; and there shall be no more death, neither sorrow, nor crying, neither shall there be any more pain: for the former things are passed away.
⁵ And he that sat upon the throne said, Behold, I make all things new. And he said unto me, Write: for these words are true and faithful.

Acceptance with Joy

Good News II

Mark 16:15-18; Revelation 2:1-29, 3:1-22 (KJV)

Mark 16:15-18 (KJV)
15 And he said unto them, Go ye into all the world, and preach the gospel to every creature.
16 He that believeth and is baptized shall be saved; but he that believeth not shall be damned.
17 And these signs shall follow them that believe; In my name shall they cast out devils; they shall speak with new tongues;
18 They shall take up serpents; and if they drink any deadly thing, it shall not hurt them; they shall lay hands on the sick, and they shall recover.

Revelation 2:1-29 (KJV)
1 Unto the angel of the church of Ephesus write; These things saith he that holdeth the seven stars in his right hand, who walketh in the midst of the seven golden candlesticks;
2 I know thy works, and thy labour, and thy patience, and how thou canst not bear them which are evil: and thou hast tried them which say they are apostles, and are not, and hast found them liars:
3 And hast borne, and hast patience, and for my name's sake hast laboured, and hast not fainted.
4 Nevertheless I have somewhat against thee, because thou hast left thy first love.
5 Remember therefore from whence thou art fallen, and repent, and do the first works; or else I will come unto thee quickly, and will remove thy candlestick out of his place, except thou repent.
6 But this thou hast, that thou hatest the deeds of the Nicolaitanes, which I also hate.

⁷ He that hath an ear, let him hear what the Spirit saith unto the churches; To him that overcometh will I give to eat of the tree of life, which is in the midst of the paradise of God.
⁸ And unto the angel of the church in Smyrna write; These things saith the first and the last, which was dead, and is alive;
⁹ I know thy works, and tribulation, and poverty, (but thou art rich) and I know the blasphemy of them which say they are Jews, and are not, but are the synagogue of Satan.
¹⁰ Fear none of those things which thou shalt suffer: behold, the devil shall cast some of you into prison, that ye may be tried; and ye shall have tribulation ten days: be thou faithful unto death, and I will give thee a crown of life.
¹¹ He that hath an ear, let him hear what the Spirit saith unto the churches; He that overcometh shall not be hurt of the second death.
¹² And to the angel of the church in Pergamos write; These things saith he which hath the sharp sword with two edges;
¹³ I know thy works, and where thou dwellest, even where Satan's seat is: and thou holdest fast my name, and hast not denied my faith, even in those days wherein Antipas was my faithful martyr, who was slain among you, where Satan dwelleth.
¹⁴ But I have a few things against thee, because thou hast there them that hold the doctrine of Balaam, who taught Balac to cast a stumblingblock before the children of Israel, to eat things sacrificed unto idols, and to commit fornication.
¹⁵ So hast thou also them that hold the doctrine of the Nicolaitanes, which thing I hate.
¹⁶ Repent; or else I will come unto thee quickly, and will fight against them with the sword of my mouth.

¹⁷ He that hath an ear, let him hear what the Spirit saith unto the churches; To him that overcometh will I give to eat of the hidden manna, and will give him a white stone, and in the stone a new name written, which no man knoweth saving he that receiveth it.
¹⁸ And unto the angel of the church in Thyatira write; These things saith the Son of God, who hath his eyes like unto a flame of fire, and his feet are like fine brass;
¹⁹ I know thy works, and charity, and service, and faith, and thy patience, and thy works; and the last to be more than the first.
²⁰ Notwithstanding I have a few things against thee, because thou sufferest that woman Jezebel, which calleth herself a prophetess, to teach and to seduce my servants to commit fornication, and to eat things sacrificed unto idols.
²¹ And I gave her space to repent of her fornication; and she repented not.
²² Behold, I will cast her into a bed, and them that commit adultery with her into great tribulation, except they repent of their deeds.
²³ And I will kill her children with death; and all the churches shall know that I am he which searcheth the reins and hearts: and I will give unto every one of you according to your works.
²⁴ But unto you I say, and unto the rest in Thyatira, as many as have not this doctrine, and which have not known the depths of Satan, as they speak; I will put upon you none other burden.
²⁵ But that which ye have already hold fast till I come.
²⁶ And he that overcometh, and keepeth my works unto the end, to him will I give power over the nations:
²⁷ And he shall rule them with a rod of iron; as the vessels of a potter shall they be broken to shivers: even as I received of my Father.

²⁸ And I will give him the morning star.
²⁹ He that hath an ear, let him hear what the Spirit saith unto the churches.

Revelation 3:1-22 (KJV)
¹ And unto the angel of the church in Sardis write; These things saith he that hath the seven Spirits of God, and the seven stars; I know thy works, that thou hast a name that thou livest, and art dead.
² Be watchful, and strengthen the things which remain, that are ready to die: for I have not found thy works perfect before God.
³ Remember therefore how thou hast received and heard, and hold fast, and repent. If therefore thou shalt not watch, I will come on thee as a thief, and thou shalt not know what hour I will come upon thee.
⁴ Thou hast a few names even in Sardis which have not defiled their garments; and they shall walk with me in white: for they are worthy.
⁵ He that overcometh, the same shall be clothed in white raiment; and I will not blot out his name out of the book of life, but I will confess his name before my Father, and before his angels.
⁶ He that hath an ear, let him hear what the Spirit saith unto the churches.
⁷ And to the angel of the church in Philadelphia write; These things saith he that is holy, he that is true, he that hath the key of David, he that openeth, and no man shutteth; and shutteth, and no man openeth;
⁸ I know thy works: behold, I have set before thee an open door, and no man can shut it: for thou hast a little strength, and hast kept my word, and hast not denied my name.

⁹ Behold, I will make them of the synagogue of Satan, which say they are Jews, and are not, but do lie; behold, I will make them to come and worship before thy feet, and to know that I have loved thee.
¹⁰ Because thou hast kept the word of my patience, I also will keep thee from the hour of temptation, which shall come upon all the world, to try them that dwell upon the earth.
¹¹ Behold, I come quickly: hold that fast which thou hast, that no man take thy crown.
¹² Him that overcometh will I make a pillar in the temple of my God, and he shall go no more out: and I will write upon him the name of my God, and the name of the city of my God, which is new Jerusalem, which cometh down out of heaven from my God: and I will write upon him my new name.
¹³ He that hath an ear, let him hear what the Spirit saith unto the churches.
¹⁴ And unto the angel of the church of the Laodiceans write; These things saith the Amen, the faithful and true witness, the beginning of the creation of God;
¹⁵ I know thy works, that thou art neither cold nor hot: I would thou wert cold or hot.
¹⁶ So then because thou art lukewarm, and neither cold nor hot, I will spue thee out of my mouth.
¹⁷ Because thou sayest, I am rich, and increased with goods, and have need of nothing; and knowest not that thou art wretched, and miserable, and poor, and blind, and naked:

¹⁸ I counsel thee to buy of me gold tried in the fire, that thou mayest be rich; and white raiment, that thou mayest be clothed, and that the shame of thy nakedness do not appear; and anoint thine eyes with eyesalve, that thou mayest see.
¹⁹ As many as I love, I rebuke and chasten: be zealous therefore, and repent.
²⁰ Behold, I stand at the door, and knock: if any man hear my voice, and open the door, I will come in to him, and will sup with him, and he with me.
²¹ To him that overcometh will I grant to sit with me in my throne, even as I also overcame, and am set down with my Father in his throne.
²² He that hath an ear, let him hear what the Spirit saith unto the churches.

It's Adoption Time

Galatians 4:5-7; Ephesians 1:4-5 (KJV)

Galatians 4:5-7 (KJV)
5 To redeem them that were under the law, that we might receive the adoption of sons.
6 And because ye are sons, God hath sent forth the Spirit of his Son into your hearts, crying, Abba, Father.
7 Wherefore thou art no more a servant, but a son; and if a son, then an heir of God through Christ.

Ephesians 1:4-5 (KJV)
4 According as he hath chosen us in him before the foundation of the world, that we should be holy and without blame before him in love:
5 Having predestinated us unto the adoption of children by Jesus Christ to himself, according to the good pleasure of his will,

It's War!

Ephesians 6:10-17 (KJV)

Ephesians 6:10-17 (KJV)
[10] Finally, my brethren, be strong in the Lord, and in the power of his might.
[11] Put on the whole armour of God, that ye may be able to stand against the wiles of the devil.
[12] For we wrestle not against flesh and blood, but against principalities, against powers, against the rulers of the darkness of this world, against spiritual wickedness in high places.
[13] Wherefore take unto you the whole armour of God, that ye may be able to withstand in the evil day, and having done all, to stand.
[14] Stand therefore, having your loins girt about with truth, and having on the breastplate of righteousness;
[15] And your feet shod with the preparation of the gospel of peace;
[16] Above all, taking the shield of faith, wherewith ye shall be able to quench all the fiery darts of the wicked.
[17] And take the helmet of salvation, and the sword of the Spirit, which is the word of God:

Joseph

Genesis 37:2-5, 9, 15, 31-35, 41:41-43, 45:1-5 (KJV)

Genesis 37:2-5 (KJV)
2 These are the generations of Jacob. Joseph, being seventeen years old, was feeding the flock with his brethren; and the lad was with the sons of Bilhah, and with the sons of Zilpah, his father's wives: and Joseph brought unto his father their evil report.
3 Now Israel loved Joseph more than all his children, because he was the son of his old age: and he made him a coat of many colours.
4 And when his brethren saw that their father loved him more than all his brethren, they hated him, and could not speak peaceably unto him.
5 And Joseph dreamed a dream, and he told it his brethren: and they hated him yet the more.

Genesis 37:9 (KJV)
9 And he dreamed yet another dream, and told it his brethren, and said, Behold, I have dreamed a dream more; and, behold, the sun and the moon and the eleven stars made obeisance to me.

Genesis 37:15 (KJV)
15 And a certain man found him, and, behold, he was wandering in the field: and the man asked him, saying, What seekest thou?

Genesis 37:31-35 (KJV)
31 And they took Joseph's coat, and killed a kid of the goats, and dipped the coat in the blood;
32 And they sent the coat of many colours, and they brought it to their father; and said, This have we found: know now whether it be thy son's coat or no.

³³ And he knew it, and said, It is my son's coat; an evil beast hath devoured him; Joseph is without doubt rent in pieces.
³⁴ And Jacob rent his clothes, and put sackcloth upon his loins, and mourned for his son many days.
³⁵ And all his sons and all his daughters rose up to comfort him; but he refused to be comforted; and he said, For I will go down into the grave unto my son mourning. Thus his father wept for him.

Genesis 41:41-43 (KJV)
⁴¹ And Pharaoh said unto Joseph, See, I have set thee over all the land of Egypt.
⁴² And Pharaoh took off his ring from his hand, and put it upon Joseph's hand, and arrayed him in vestures of fine linen, and put a gold chain about his neck;
⁴³ And he made him to ride in the second chariot which he had; and they cried before him, Bow the knee: and he made him ruler over all the land of Egypt.

Genesis 45:1-5 (KJV)
¹Then Joseph could not refrain himself before all them that stood by him; and he cried, Cause every man to go out from me. And there stood no man with him, while Joseph made himself known unto his brethren.
² And he wept aloud: and the Egyptians and the house of Pharaoh heard.
³ And Joseph said unto his brethren, I am Joseph; doth my father yet live? And his brethren could not answer him; for they were troubled at his presence.

Acceptance with Joy

⁴ And Joseph said unto his brethren, Come near to me, I pray you. And they came near. And he said, I am Joseph your brother, whom ye sold into Egypt.
⁵ Now therefore be not grieved, nor angry with yourselves, that ye sold me hither: for God did send me before you to preserve life.

Just Do It!

Mark 16:15-20 (KJV)

Mark 16:15-20 (KJV)
15 And he said unto them, Go ye into all the world, and preach the gospel to every creature.
16 He that believeth and is baptized shall be saved; but he that believeth not shall be damned.
17 And these signs shall follow them that believe; In my name shall they cast out devils; they shall speak with new tongues;
18 They shall take up serpents; and if they drink any deadly thing, it shall not hurt them; they shall lay hands on the sick, and they shall recover.
19 So then after the Lord had spoken unto them, he was received up into heaven, and sat on the right hand of God.
20 And they went forth, and preached every where, the Lord working with them, and confirming the word with signs following. Amen.

Acceptance with Joy

Master of Masters

Matthew 4:1, 4:19, 5:1, 7:29, 8:26, 11:5; Luke 8:43-48;
John 2:1-11, 11:43-44 (KJV)

Matthew 4:1 (KJV)
1 Then was Jesus led up of the Spirit into the wilderness to be tempted of the devil.

Matthew 4:19 (KJV)
19 And he saith unto them, Follow me, and I will make you fishers of men.

Matthew 5:1 (KJV)
1 And seeing the multitudes, he went up into a mountain: and when he was set, his disciples came unto him:

Matthew 7:29 (KJV)
29 For he taught them as one having authority, and not as the scribes.

Matthew 8:26 (KJV)
26 And he saith unto them, Why are ye fearful, O ye of little faith? Then he arose, and rebuked the winds and the sea; and there was a great calm.

Matthew 11:5 (KJV)
5 The blind receive their sight, and the lame walk, the lepers are cleansed, and the deaf hear, the dead are raised up, and the poor have the gospel preached to them.

Luke 8:43-48 (KJV)
43 And a woman having an issue of blood twelve years, which had spent all her living upon physicians, neither could be healed of any,
44 Came behind him, and touched the border of his garment: and immediately her issue of blood stanched.

⁴⁵ And Jesus said, Who touched me? When all denied, Peter and they that were with him said, Master, the multitude throng thee and press thee, and sayest thou, Who touched me?
⁴⁶ And Jesus said, Somebody hath touched me: for I perceive that virtue is gone out of me.
⁴⁷ And when the woman saw that she was not hid, she came trembling, and falling down before him, she declared unto him before all the people for what cause she had touched him, and how she was healed immediately.
⁴⁸ And he said unto her, Daughter, be of good comfort: thy faith hath made thee whole; go in peace.

John 2:1-11 (KJV)
¹ And the third day there was a marriage in Cana of Galilee; and the mother of Jesus was there:
² And both Jesus was called, and his disciples, to the marriage.
³ And when they wanted wine, the mother of Jesus saith unto him, They have no wine.
⁴ Jesus saith unto her, Woman, what have I to do with thee? mine hour is not yet come.
⁵ His mother saith unto the servants, Whatsoever he saith unto you, do it.
⁶ And there were set there six waterpots of stone, after the manner of the purifying of the Jews, containing two or three firkins apiece.
⁷ Jesus saith unto them, Fill the waterpots with water. And they filled them up to the brim.
⁸ And he saith unto them, Draw out now, and bear unto the governor of the feast. And they bare it.

⁹ When the ruler of the feast had tasted the water that was made wine, and knew not whence it was: (but the servants which drew the water knew;) the governor of the feast called the bridegroom,
¹⁰ And saith unto him, Every man at the beginning doth set forth good wine; and when men have well drunk, then that which is worse: but thou hast kept the good wine until now.
¹¹ This beginning of miracles did Jesus in Cana of Galilee, and manifested forth his glory; and his disciples believed on him.

John 11:43-44 (KJV)
⁴³ And when he thus had spoken, he cried with a loud voice, Lazarus, come forth.
⁴⁴ And he that was dead came forth, bound hand and foot with graveclothes: and his face was bound about with a napkin. Jesus saith unto them, Loose him, and let him go.

Dr. Lydia A. Woods

No Abundance in the Wilderness

Matthew 4:1-11 (KJV)

Matthew 4:1-11 (KJV)
¹Then was Jesus led up of the Spirit into the wilderness to be tempted of the devil.
² And when he had fasted forty days and forty nights, he was afterward an hungred.
³ And when the tempter came to him, he said, If thou be the Son of God, command that these stones be made bread.
⁴ But he answered and said, It is written, Man shall not live by bread alone, but by every word that proceedeth out of the mouth of God.
⁵ Then the devil taketh him up into the holy city, and setteth him on a pinnacle of the temple,
⁶ And saith unto him, If thou be the Son of God, cast thyself down: for it is written, He shall give his angels charge concerning thee: and in their hands they shall bear thee up, lest at any time thou dash thy foot against a stone.
⁷ Jesus said unto him, It is written again, Thou shalt not tempt the Lord thy God.
⁸ Again, the devil taketh him up into an exceeding high mountain, and sheweth him all the kingdoms of the world, and the glory of them;
⁹ And saith unto him, All these things will I give thee, if thou wilt fall down and worship me.
¹⁰ Then saith Jesus unto him, Get thee hence, Satan: for it is written, Thou shalt worship the Lord thy God, and him only shalt thou serve.
¹¹ Then the devil leaveth him, and, behold, angels came and ministered unto him.

Put It All On!

Ephesians 6:11-17 (KJV)

Ephesians 6:11-17 (KJV)
[11] Put on the whole armour of God, that ye may be able to stand against the wiles of the devil.
[12] For we wrestle not against flesh and blood, but against principalities, against powers, against the rulers of the darkness of this world, against spiritual wickedness in high places.
[13] Wherefore take unto you the whole armour of God, that ye may be able to withstand in the evil day, and having done all, to stand.
[14] Stand therefore, having your loins girt about with truth, and having on the breastplate of righteousness;
[15] And your feet shod with the preparation of the gospel of peace;
[16] Above all, taking the shield of faith, wherewith ye shall be able to quench all the fiery darts of the wicked.
[17] And take the helmet of salvation, and the sword of the Spirit, which is the word of God:

Dr. Lydia A. Woods

Quest for Salvation

Malachi 3:13-18 (KJV)

Malachi 3:13-18 (KJV)
[13] Your words have been stout against me, saith the LORD. Yet ye say, What have we spoken so much against thee?
[14] Ye have said, It is vain to serve God: and what profit is it that we have kept his ordinance, and that we have walked mournfully before the LORD of hosts?
[15] And now we call the proud happy; yea, they that work wickedness are set up; yea, they that tempt God are even delivered.
[16] Then they that feared the LORD spake often one to another: and the LORD hearkened, and heard it, and a book of remembrance was written before him for them that feared the LORD, and that thought upon his name.
[17] And they shall be mine, saith the LORD of hosts, in that day when I make up my jewels; and I will spare them, as a man spareth his own son that serveth him.
[18] Then shall ye return, and discern between the righteous and the wicked, between him that serveth God and him that serveth him not.

Simply Because You Are Mine

Matthew 7:11; I Corinthians 2:9-11; Isaiah 64:4;
Psalm 31:19 (KJV)

Matthew 7:11 (KJV)
11 If ye then, being evil, know how to give good gifts unto your children, how much more shall your Father which is in heaven give good things to them that ask him?

I Corinthians 2:9-11 (KJV)
9 But as it is written, Eye hath not seen, nor ear heard, neither have entered into the heart of man, the things which God hath prepared for them that love him.
10 But God hath revealed them unto us by his Spirit: for the Spirit searcheth all things, yea, the deep things of God.
11 For what man knoweth the things of a man, save the spirit of man which is in him? even so the things of God knoweth no man, but the Spirit of God.

Isaiah 64:4 (KJV)
4 For since the beginning of the world men have not heard, nor perceived by the ear, neither hath the eye seen, O God, beside thee, what he hath prepared for him that waiteth for him.

Psalm 31:19 (KJV)
19 Oh how great is thy goodness, which thou hast laid up for them that fear thee; which thou hast wrought for them that trust in thee before the sons of men!

Dr. Lydia A. Woods

So Be Like Job

Job 2:13 (KJV)

Job 2:13 (KJV)
[13] So they sat down with him upon the ground seven days and seven nights, and none spake a word unto him: for they saw that his grief was very great.

What's His Face?

Genesis 3:15; John 19:11 (KJV)

Genesis 3:15 (KJV)
15 And I will put enmity between thee and the woman, and between thy seed and her seed; it shall bruise thy head, and thou shalt bruise his heel.

John 19:11 (KJV)
11 Jesus answered, Thou couldest have no power at all against me, except it were given thee from above: therefore he that delivered me unto thee hath the greater sin.

For the Edification of the Saints

Adult vs Child

Matthew 18:3; Proverbs 22:6; Luke 18:16 (KJV)

Matthew 18:3 (KJV)
3 And said, Verily I say unto you, Except ye be converted, and become as little children, ye shall not enter into the kingdom of heaven.

Proverbs 22:6 (KJV)
6 Train up a child in the way he should go: and when he is old, he will not depart from it.

Luke 18:16 (KJV)
16 But Jesus called them unto him, and said, Suffer little children to come unto me, and forbid them not: for of such is the kingdom of God.

Dr. Lydia A. Woods

But For Your Praying Saints

Ephesians 6:18; I Thessalonians 5:17; James 5:16 (KJV)

Ephesians 6:18 (KJV)
18 Praying always with all prayer and supplication in the Spirit, and watching thereunto with all perseverance and supplication for all saints;

I Thessalonians 5:17 (KJV)
17 Pray without ceasing.

James 5:16 (KJV)
16 Confess your faults one to another, and pray one for another, that ye may be healed. The effectual fervent prayer of a righteous man availeth much.

Created in My Father's Image

Philippians 2:6; Galatians 4:6 (KJV)

Philippians 2:6 (KJV)
6 Who, being in the form of God, thought it not robbery to be equal with God:

Galatians 4:6 (KJV)
6 And because ye are sons, God hath sent forth the Spirit of his Son into your hearts, crying, Abba, Father.

Don't Envy Those

Malachi 3:13-18 (KJV)

Malachi 3:13-18 (KJV)
[13] Your words have been stout against me, saith the LORD. Yet ye say, What have we spoken so much against thee?
[14] Ye have said, It is vain to serve God: and what profit is it that we have kept his ordinance, and that we have walked mournfully before the LORD of hosts?
[15] And now we call the proud happy; yea, they that work wickedness are set up; yea, they that tempt God are even delivered.
[16] Then they that feared the LORD spake often one to another: and the LORD hearkened, and heard it, and a book of remembrance was written before him for them that feared the LORD, and that thought upon his name.
[17] And they shall be mine, saith the LORD of hosts, in that day when I make up my jewels; and I will spare them, as a man spareth his own son that serveth him.
[18] Then shall ye return, and discern between the righteous and the wicked, between him that serveth God and him that serveth him not.

The Family Business

I Corinthians 3:7-9 (KJV)

I Corinthians 3:7-9 (KJV)
⁷ So then neither is he that planteth any thing, neither he that watereth; but God that giveth the increase.
⁸ Now he that planteth and he that watereth are one: and every man shall receive his own reward according to his own labour.
⁹ For we are labourers together with God: ye are God's husbandry, ye are God's building.

Fear vs Faith

I John 4:18; Romans 8:15; Luke 12:32; Psalm 118:6 (KJV)

I John 4:18 (KJV)
18 There is no fear in love; but perfect love casteth out fear: because fear hath torment. He that feareth is not made perfect in love.

Romans 8:15 (KJV)
15 For ye have not received the spirit of bondage again to fear; but ye have received the Spirit of adoption, whereby we cry, Abba, Father.

Luke 12:32 (KJV)
32 Fear not, little flock; for it is your Father's good pleasure to give you the kingdom.

Psalm 118:6 (KJV)
6 The LORD is on my side; I will not fear: what can man do unto me?

Go the Distance

Revelation 2:1-29, 3:1-22 (KJV)

Revelation 2:1-29 (KJV)

1 Unto the angel of the church of Ephesus write; These things saith he that holdeth the seven stars in his right hand, who walketh in the midst of the seven golden candlesticks;
2 I know thy works, and thy labour, and thy patience, and how thou canst not bear them which are evil: and thou hast tried them which say they are apostles, and are not, and hast found them liars:
3 And hast borne, and hast patience, and for my name's sake hast laboured, and hast not fainted.
4 Nevertheless I have somewhat against thee, because thou hast left thy first love.
5 Remember therefore from whence thou art fallen, and repent, and do the first works; or else I will come unto thee quickly, and will remove thy candlestick out of his place, except thou repent.
6 But this thou hast, that thou hatest the deeds of the Nicolaitanes, which I also hate.
7 He that hath an ear, let him hear what the Spirit saith unto the churches; To him that overcometh will I give to eat of the tree of life, which is in the midst of the paradise of God.
8 And unto the angel of the church in Smyrna write; These things saith the first and the last, which was dead, and is alive;
9 I know thy works, and tribulation, and poverty, (but thou art rich) and I know the blasphemy of them which say they are Jews, and are not, but are the synagogue of Satan.
10 Fear none of those things which thou shalt suffer: behold, the devil shall cast some of you into prison, that ye may be tried; and ye shall have tribulation ten days: be thou faithful unto death, and I will give thee a crown of life.

¹¹ He that hath an ear, let him hear what the Spirit saith unto the churches; He that overcometh shall not be hurt of the second death.
¹² And to the angel of the church in Pergamos write; These things saith he which hath the sharp sword with two edges;
¹³ I know thy works, and where thou dwellest, even where Satan's seat is: and thou holdest fast my name, and hast not denied my faith, even in those days wherein Antipas was my faithful martyr, who was slain among you, where Satan dwelleth.
¹⁴ But I have a few things against thee, because thou hast there them that hold the doctrine of Balaam, who taught Balac to cast a stumblingblock before the children of Israel, to eat things sacrificed unto idols, and to commit fornication.
¹⁵ So hast thou also them that hold the doctrine of the Nicolaitanes, which thing I hate.
¹⁶ Repent; or else I will come unto thee quickly, and will fight against them with the sword of my mouth.
¹⁷ He that hath an ear, let him hear what the Spirit saith unto the churches; To him that overcometh will I give to eat of the hidden manna, and will give him a white stone, and in the stone a new name written, which no man knoweth saving he that receiveth it.
¹⁸ And unto the angel of the church in Thyatira write; These things saith the Son of God, who hath his eyes like unto a flame of fire, and his feet are like fine brass;
¹⁹ I know thy works, and charity, and service, and faith, and thy patience, and thy works; and the last to be more than the first.
²⁰ Notwithstanding I have a few things against thee, because thou sufferest that woman Jezebel, which calleth herself a prophetess, to teach and to seduce my servants to commit fornication, and to eat things sacrificed unto idols.

21 And I gave her space to repent of her fornication; and she repented not.
22 Behold, I will cast her into a bed, and them that commit adultery with her into great tribulation, except they repent of their deeds.
23 And I will kill her children with death; and all the churches shall know that I am he which searcheth the reins and hearts: and I will give unto every one of you according to your works.
24 But unto you I say, and unto the rest in Thyatira, as many as have not this doctrine, and which have not known the depths of Satan, as they speak; I will put upon you none other burden.
25 But that which ye have already hold fast till I come.
26 And he that overcometh, and keepeth my works unto the end, to him will I give power over the nations:
27 And he shall rule them with a rod of iron; as the vessels of a potter shall they be broken to shivers: even as I received of my Father.
28 And I will give him the morning star.
29 He that hath an ear, let him hear what the Spirit saith unto the churches.

Revelation 3:1-22 (KJV)
1 And unto the angel of the church in Sardis write; These things saith he that hath the seven Spirits of God, and the seven stars; I know thy works, that thou hast a name that thou livest, and art dead.
2 Be watchful, and strengthen the things which remain, that are ready to die: for I have not found thy works perfect before God.

³ Remember therefore how thou hast received and heard, and hold fast, and repent. If therefore thou shalt not watch, I will come on thee as a thief, and thou shalt not know what hour I will come upon thee.

⁴ Thou hast a few names even in Sardis which have not defiled their garments; and they shall walk with me in white: for they are worthy.

⁵ He that overcometh, the same shall be clothed in white raiment; and I will not blot out his name out of the book of life, but I will confess his name before my Father, and before his angels.

⁶ He that hath an ear, let him hear what the Spirit saith unto the churches.

⁷ And to the angel of the church in Philadelphia write; These things saith he that is holy, he that is true, he that hath the key of David, he that openeth, and no man shutteth; and shutteth, and no man openeth;

⁸ I know thy works: behold, I have set before thee an open door, and no man can shut it: for thou hast a little strength, and hast kept my word, and hast not denied my name.

⁹ Behold, I will make them of the synagogue of Satan, which say they are Jews, and are not, but do lie; behold, I will make them to come and worship before thy feet, and to know that I have loved thee.

¹⁰ Because thou hast kept the word of my patience, I also will keep thee from the hour of temptation, which shall come upon all the world, to try them that dwell upon the earth.

¹¹ Behold, I come quickly: hold that fast which thou hast, that no man take thy crown.

Acceptance with Joy

¹² Him that overcometh will I make a pillar in the temple of my God, and he shall go no more out: and I will write upon him the name of my God, and the name of the city of my God, which is new Jerusalem, which cometh down out of heaven from my God: and I will write upon him my new name.

¹³ He that hath an ear, let him hear what the Spirit saith unto the churches.

¹⁴ And unto the angel of the church of the Laodiceans write; These things saith the Amen, the faithful and true witness, the beginning of the creation of God;

¹⁵ I know thy works, that thou art neither cold nor hot: I would thou wert cold or hot.

¹⁶ So then because thou art lukewarm, and neither cold nor hot, I will spue thee out of my mouth.

¹⁷ Because thou sayest, I am rich, and increased with goods, and have need of nothing; and knowest not that thou art wretched, and miserable, and poor, and blind, and naked:

¹⁸ I counsel thee to buy of me gold tried in the fire, that thou mayest be rich; and white raiment, that thou mayest be clothed, and that the shame of thy nakedness do not appear; and anoint thine eyes with eyesalve, that thou mayest see.

¹⁹ As many as I love, I rebuke and chasten: be zealous therefore, and repent.

²⁰ Behold, I stand at the door, and knock: if any man hear my voice, and open the door, I will come in to him, and will sup with him, and he with me.

[21] To him that overcometh will I grant to sit with me in my throne, even as I also overcame, and am set down with my Father in his throne.

[22] He that hath an ear, let him hear what the Spirit saith unto the churches.

God Will Provide

Genesis 22:1-19 (KJV)

Genesis 22:1-19 (KJV)
¹ And it came to pass after these things, that God did tempt Abraham, and said unto him, Abraham: and he said, Behold, here I am.
² And he said, Take now thy son, thine only son Isaac, whom thou lovest, and get thee into the land of Moriah; and offer him there for a burnt offering upon one of the mountains which I will tell thee of.
³ And Abraham rose up early in the morning, and saddled his ass, and took two of his young men with him, and Isaac his son, and clave the wood for the burnt offering, and rose up, and went unto the place of which God had told him.
⁴ Then on the third day Abraham lifted up his eyes, and saw the place afar off.
⁵ And Abraham said unto his young men, Abide ye here with the ass; and I and the lad will go yonder and worship, and come again to you.
⁶ And Abraham took the wood of the burnt offering, and laid it upon Isaac his son; and he took the fire in his hand, and a knife; and they went both of them together.
⁷ And Isaac spake unto Abraham his father, and said, My father: and he said, Here am I, my son. And he said, Behold the fire and the wood: but where is the lamb for a burnt offering?
⁸ And Abraham said, My son, God will provide himself a lamb for a burnt offering: so they went both of them together.
⁹ And they came to the place which God had told him of; and Abraham built an altar there, and laid the wood in order, and bound Isaac his son, and laid him on the altar upon the wood.
¹⁰ And Abraham stretched forth his hand, and took the knife to slay his son.

¹¹ And the angel of the LORD called unto him out of heaven, and said, Abraham, Abraham: and he said, Here am I.
¹² And he said, Lay not thine hand upon the lad, neither do thou any thing unto him: for now I know that thou fearest God, seeing thou hast not withheld thy son, thine only son from me.
¹³ And Abraham lifted up his eyes, and looked, and behold behind him a ram caught in a thicket by his horns: and Abraham went and took the ram, and offered him up for a burnt offering in the stead of his son.
¹⁴ And Abraham called the name of that place Jehovahjireh: as it is said to this day, In the mount of the LORD it shall be seen.
¹⁵ And the angel of the LORD called unto Abraham out of heaven the second time,
¹⁶ And said, By myself have I sworn, saith the LORD, for because thou hast done this thing, and hast not withheld thy son, thine only son:
¹⁷ That in blessing I will bless thee, and in multiplying I will multiply thy seed as the stars of the heaven, and as the sand which is upon the sea shore; and thy seed shall possess the gate of his enemies;
¹⁸ And in thy seed shall all the nations of the earth be blessed; because thou hast obeyed my voice.
¹⁹ So Abraham returned unto his young men, and they rose up and went together to Beersheba; and Abraham dwelt at Beersheba.

Group Three

Matthew 8:12, 13:37-43; Luke 13:24-30 (KJV)

Matthew 8:12 (KJV)
12 But the children of the kingdom shall be cast out into outer darkness: there shall be weeping and gnashing of teeth.

Matthew 13:37-43 (KJV)
37 He answered and said unto them, He that soweth the good seed is the Son of man;
38 The field is the world; the good seed are the children of the kingdom; but the tares are the children of the wicked one;
39 The enemy that sowed them is the devil; the harvest is the end of the world; and the reapers are the angels.
40 As therefore the tares are gathered and burned in the fire; so shall it be in the end of this world.
41 The Son of man shall send forth his angels, and they shall gather out of his kingdom all things that offend, and them which do iniquity;
42 And shall cast them into a furnace of fire: there shall be wailing and gnashing of teeth.
43 Then shall the righteous shine forth as the sun in the kingdom of their Father. Who hath ears to hear, let him hear.

Luke 13:24-30 (KJV)
24 Strive to enter in at the strait gate: for many, I say unto you, will seek to enter in, and shall not be able.
25 When once the master of the house is risen up, and hath shut to the door, and ye begin to stand without, and to knock at the door, saying, Lord, Lord, open unto us; and he shall answer and say unto you, I know you not whence ye are:
26 Then shall ye begin to say, We have eaten and drunk in thy presence, and thou hast taught in our streets.

Dr. Lydia A. Woods

²⁷ But he shall say, I tell you, I know you not whence ye are; depart from me, all ye workers of iniquity.
²⁸ There shall be weeping and gnashing of teeth, when ye shall see Abraham, and Isaac, and Jacob, and all the prophets, in the kingdom of God, and you yourselves thrust out.
²⁹ And they shall come from the east, and from the west, and from the north, and from the south, and shall sit down in the kingdom of God.
³⁰ And, behold, there are last which shall be first, and there are first which shall be last.

Acceptance with Joy

Hedge of Protection

Psalm 91:1-16; I Peter 3:4-6 (KJV)

Psalm 91:1-16 (KJV)
1 He that dwelleth in the secret place of the most High shall abide under the shadow of the Almighty.
2 I will say of the LORD, He is my refuge and my fortress: my God; in him will I trust.
3 Surely he shall deliver thee from the snare of the fowler, and from the noisome pestilence.
4 He shall cover thee with his feathers, and under his wings shalt thou trust: his truth shall be thy shield and buckler.
5 Thou shalt not be afraid for the terror by night; nor for the arrow that flieth by day;
6 Nor for the pestilence that walketh in darkness; nor for the destruction that wasteth at noonday.
7 A thousand shall fall at thy side, and ten thousand at thy right hand; but it shall not come nigh thee.
8 Only with thine eyes shalt thou behold and see the reward of the wicked.
9 Because thou hast made the LORD, which is my refuge, even the most High, thy habitation;
10 There shall no evil befall thee, neither shall any plague come nigh thy dwelling.
11 For he shall give his angels charge over thee, to keep thee in all thy ways.
12 They shall bear thee up in their hands, lest thou dash thy foot against a stone.
13 Thou shalt tread upon the lion and adder: the young lion and the dragon shalt thou trample under feet.
14 Because he hath set his love upon me, therefore will I deliver him: I will set him on high, because he hath known my name.

¹⁵ He shall call upon me, and I will answer him: I will be with him in trouble; I will deliver him, and honour him.
¹⁶ With long life will I satisfy him, and shew him my salvation.

I Peter 3:4-6 (KJV)
⁴ But let it be the hidden man of the heart, in that which is not corruptible, even the ornament of a meek and quiet spirit, which is in the sight of God of great price.
⁵ For after this manner in the old time the holy women also, who trusted in God, adorned themselves, being in subjection unto their own husbands:
⁶ Even as Sara obeyed Abraham, calling him lord: whose daughters ye are, as long as ye do well, and are not afraid with any amazement.

Acceptance with Joy

How Many Times

Philippians 4:19 (KJV)

Philippians 4:19 (KJV)
19 But my God shall supply all your need according to his riches in glory by Christ Jesus.

Dr. Lydia A. Woods

How Will I Know Him?

Genesis 24:1-67 (KJV)

Genesis 24:1-67 (KJV)
¹ And Abraham was old, and well stricken in age: and the LORD had blessed Abraham in all things.
² And Abraham said unto his eldest servant of his house, that ruled over all that he had, Put, I pray thee, thy hand under my thigh:
³ And I will make thee swear by the LORD, the God of heaven, and the God of the earth, that thou shalt not take a wife unto my son of the daughters of the Canaanites, among whom I dwell:
⁴ But thou shalt go unto my country, and to my kindred, and take a wife unto my son Isaac.
⁵ And the servant said unto him, Peradventure the woman will not be willing to follow me unto this land: must I needs bring thy son again unto the land from whence thou camest?
⁶ And Abraham said unto him, Beware thou that thou bring not my son thither again.
⁷ The LORD God of heaven, which took me from my father's house, and from the land of my kindred, and which spake unto me, and that sware unto me, saying, Unto thy seed will I give this land; he shall send his angel before thee, and thou shalt take a wife unto my son from thence.
⁸ And if the woman will not be willing to follow thee, then thou shalt be clear from this my oath: only bring not my son thither again.
⁹ And the servant put his hand under the thigh of Abraham his master, and sware to him concerning that matter.
¹⁰ And the servant took ten camels of the camels of his master, and departed; for all the goods of his master were in his hand: and he arose, and went to Mesopotamia, unto the city of Nahor.

¹¹ And he made his camels to kneel down without the city by a well of water at the time of the evening, even the time that women go out to draw water.
¹² And he said O Lord God of my master Abraham, I pray thee, send me good speed this day, and shew kindness unto my master Abraham.
¹³ Behold, I stand here by the well of water; and the daughters of the men of the city come out to draw water:
¹⁴ And let it come to pass, that the damsel to whom I shall say, Let down thy pitcher, I pray thee, that I may drink; and she shall say, Drink, and I will give thy camels drink also: let the same be she that thou hast appointed for thy servant Isaac; and thereby shall I know that thou hast shewed kindness unto my master.
¹⁵ And it came to pass, before he had done speaking, that, behold, Rebekah came out, who was born to Bethuel, son of Milcah, the wife of Nahor, Abraham's brother, with her pitcher upon her shoulder.
¹⁶ And the damsel was very fair to look upon, a virgin, neither had any man known her: and she went down to the well, and filled her pitcher, and came up.
¹⁷ And the servant ran to meet her, and said, Let me, I pray thee, drink a little water of thy pitcher.
¹⁸ And she said, Drink, my lord: and she hasted, and let down her pitcher upon her hand, and gave him drink.
¹⁹ And when she had done giving him drink, she said, I will draw water for thy camels also, until they have done drinking.
²⁰ And she hasted, and emptied her pitcher into the trough, and ran again unto the well to draw water, and drew for all his camels.

²¹ And the man wondering at her held his peace, to wit whether the LORD had made his journey prosperous or not.
²² And it came to pass, as the camels had done drinking, that the man took a golden earring of half a shekel weight, and two bracelets for her hands of ten shekels weight of gold;
²³ And said, Whose daughter art thou? tell me, I pray thee: is there room in thy father's house for us to lodge in?
²⁴ And she said unto him, I am the daughter of Bethuel the son of Milcah, which she bare unto Nahor.
²⁵ She said moreover unto him, We have both straw and provender enough, and room to lodge in.
²⁶ And the man bowed down his head, and worshipped the LORD.
²⁷ And he said, Blessed be the LORD God of my master Abraham, who hath not left destitute my master of his mercy and his truth: I being in the way, the LORD led me to the house of my master's brethren.
²⁸ And the damsel ran, and told them of her mother's house these things.
²⁹ And Rebekah had a brother, and his name was Laban: and Laban ran out unto the man, unto the well.
³⁰ And it came to pass, when he saw the earring and bracelets upon his sister's hands, and when he heard the words of Rebekah his sister, saying, Thus spake the man unto me; that he came unto the man; and, behold, he stood by the camels at the well.
³¹ And he said, Come in, thou blessed of the LORD; wherefore standest thou without? for I have prepared the house, and room for the camels.

Acceptance with Joy

³² And the man came into the house: and he ungirded his camels, and gave straw and provender for the camels, and water to wash his feet, and the men's feet that were with him.

³³ And there was set meat before him to eat: but he said, I will not eat, until I have told mine errand. And he said, Speak on.

³⁴ And he said, I am Abraham's servant.

³⁵ And the LORD hath blessed my master greatly; and he is become great: and he hath given him flocks, and herds, and silver, and gold, and menservants, and maidservants, and camels, and asses.

³⁶ And Sarah my master's wife bare a son to my master when she was old: and unto him hath he given all that he hath.

³⁷ And my master made me swear, saying, Thou shalt not take a wife to my son of the daughters of the Canaanites, in whose land I dwell:

³⁸ But thou shalt go unto my father's house, and to my kindred, and take a wife unto my son.

³⁹ And I said unto my master, Peradventure the woman will not follow me.

⁴⁰ And he said unto me, The LORD, before whom I walk, will send his angel with thee, and prosper thy way; and thou shalt take a wife for my son of my kindred, and of my father's house:

⁴¹ Then shalt thou be clear from this my oath, when thou comest to my kindred; and if they give not thee one, thou shalt be clear from my oath.

⁴² And I came this day unto the well, and said, O LORD God of my master Abraham, if now thou do prosper my way which I go:

⁴³ Behold, I stand by the well of water; and it shall come to pass, that when the virgin cometh forth to draw water, and I say to her, Give me, I pray thee, a little water of thy pitcher to drink;

⁴⁴ And she say to me, Both drink thou, and I will also draw for thy camels: let the same be the woman whom the Lord hath appointed out for my master's son.

⁴⁵ And before I had done speaking in mine heart, behold, Rebekah came forth with her pitcher on her shoulder; and she went down unto the well, and drew water: and I said unto her, Let me drink, I pray thee.

⁴⁶ And she made haste, and let down her pitcher from her shoulder, and said, Drink, and I will give thy camels drink also: so I drank, and she made the camels drink also.

⁴⁷ And I asked her, and said, Whose daughter art thou? And she said, the daughter of Bethuel, Nahor's son, whom Milcah bare unto him: and I put the earring upon her face, and the bracelets upon her hands.

⁴⁸ And I bowed down my head, and worshipped the Lord, and blessed the Lord God of my master Abraham, which had led me in the right way to take my master's brother's daughter unto his son.

⁴⁹ And now if ye will deal kindly and truly with my master, tell me: and if not, tell me; that I may turn to the right hand, or to the left.

⁵⁰ Then Laban and Bethuel answered and said, The thing proceedeth from the Lord: we cannot speak unto thee bad or good.

⁵¹ Behold, Rebekah is before thee, take her, and go, and let her be thy master's son's wife, as the Lord hath spoken.

⁵² And it came to pass, that, when Abraham's servant heard their words, he worshipped the Lord, bowing himself to the earth.

⁵³ And the servant brought forth jewels of silver, and jewels of gold, and raiment, and gave them to Rebekah: he gave also to her brother and to her mother precious things.

Acceptance with Joy

⁵⁴ And they did eat and drink, he and the men that were with him, and tarried all night; and they rose up in the morning, and he said, Send me away unto my master.
⁵⁵ And her brother and her mother said, Let the damsel abide with us a few days, at the least ten; after that she shall go.
⁵⁶ And he said unto them, Hinder me not, seeing the LORD hath prospered my way; send me away that I may go to my master.
⁵⁷ And they said, We will call the damsel, and enquire at her mouth.
⁵⁸ And they called Rebekah, and said unto her, Wilt thou go with this man? And she said, I will go.
⁵⁹ And they sent away Rebekah their sister, and her nurse, and Abraham's servant, and his men.
⁶⁰ And they blessed Rebekah, and said unto her, Thou art our sister, be thou the mother of thousands of millions, and let thy seed possess the gate of those which hate them.
⁶¹ And Rebekah arose, and her damsels, and they rode upon the camels, and followed the man: and the servant took Rebekah, and went his way.
⁶² And Isaac came from the way of the well Lahairoi; for he dwelt in the south country.
⁶³ And Isaac went out to meditate in the field at the eventide: and he lifted up his eyes, and saw, and, behold, the camels were coming.
⁶⁴ And Rebekah lifted up her eyes, and when she saw Isaac, she lighted off the camel.
⁶⁵ For she had said unto the servant, What man is this that walketh in the field to meet us? And the servant had said, It is my master: therefore she took a vail, and covered herself.
⁶⁶ And the servant told Isaac all things that he had done.

⁶⁷ And Isaac brought her into his mother Sarah's tent, and took Rebekah, and she became his wife; and he loved her: and Isaac was comforted after his mother's death.

I Need the Eyes of Jesus

Luke 4:18; Psalm 119:105; I Corinthians 3:16 (KJV)

Luke 4:18 (KJV)
18 The Spirit of the Lord is upon me, because he hath anointed me to preach the gospel to the poor; he hath sent me to heal the brokenhearted, to preach deliverance to the captives, and recovering of sight to the blind, to set at liberty them that are bruised,

Psalm 119:105 (KJV)
105 Thy word is a lamp unto my feet, and a light unto my path.

I Corinthians 3:16 (KJV)
16 Know ye not that ye are the temple of God, and that the Spirit of God dwelleth in you?

Dr. Lydia A. Woods

If You Want to Make God Laugh!

Proverbs 19:21; Matthew 5:36; Isaiah 46:9-11 (KJV)

Proverbs 19:21 (KJV)
21 There are many devices in a man's heart; nevertheless the counsel of the LORD, that shall stand.

Matthew 5:36 (KJV)
36 Neither shalt thou swear by thy head, because thou canst not make one hair white or black.

Isaiah 46:9-11 (KJV)
9 Remember the former things of old: for I am God, and there is none else; I am God, and there is none like me,
10 Declaring the end from the beginning, and from ancient times the things that are not yet done, saying, My counsel shall stand, and I will do all my pleasure:
11 Calling a ravenous bird from the east, the man that executeth my counsel from a far country: yea, I have spoken it, I will also bring it to pass; I have purposed it, I will also do it.

In a Split Second

James 1:8; II Corinthians 10:5 (KJV)

James 1:8 (KJV)
⁸ A double minded man is unstable in all his ways.

II Corinthians 10:5 (KJV)
⁵ Casting down imaginations, and every high thing that exalteth itself against the knowledge of God, and bringing into captivity every thought to the obedience of Christ;

Dr. Lydia A. Woods

The Inside of the Cup

Matthew 23:25; Luke 11:39 (KJV)

Matthew 23:25 (KJV)
25 Woe unto you, scribes and Pharisees, hypocrites! for ye make clean the outside of the cup and of the platter, but within they are full of extortion and excess.

Luke 11:39 (KJV)
39 And the Lord said unto him, Now do ye Pharisees make clean the outside of the cup and the platter; but your inward part is full of ravening and wickedness.

It's Not About Money

Luke 12:22-34; Matthew 6:25-34 (KJV)

Luke 12:22-34 (KJV)
22 And he said unto his disciples, Therefore I say unto you, Take no thought for your life, what ye shall eat; neither for the body, what ye shall put on.
23 The life is more than meat, and the body is more than raiment.
24 Consider the ravens: for they neither sow nor reap; which neither have storehouse nor barn; and God feedeth them: how much more are ye better than the fowls?
25 And which of you with taking thought can add to his stature one cubit?
26 If ye then be not able to do that thing which is least, why take ye thought for the rest?
27 Consider the lilies how they grow: they toil not, they spin not; and yet I say unto you, that Solomon in all his glory was not arrayed like one of these.
28 If then God so clothe the grass, which is to day in the field, and to morrow is cast into the oven; how much more will he clothe you, O ye of little faith?
29 And seek not ye what ye shall eat, or what ye shall drink, neither be ye of doubtful mind.
30 For all these things do the nations of the world seek after: and your Father knoweth that ye have need of these things.
31 But rather seek ye the kingdom of God; and all these things shall be added unto you.
32 Fear not, little flock; for it is your Father's good pleasure to give you the kingdom.
33 Sell that ye have, and give alms; provide yourselves bags which wax not old, a treasure in the heavens that faileth not, where no thief approacheth, neither moth corrupteth.

³⁴ For where your treasure is, there will your heart be also.

Matthew 6:25-34 (KJV)
²⁵ Therefore I say unto you, Take no thought for your life, what ye shall eat, or what ye shall drink; nor yet for your body, what ye shall put on. Is not the life more than meat, and the body than raiment?
²⁶ Behold the fowls of the air: for they sow not, neither do they reap, nor gather into barns; yet your heavenly Father feedeth them. Are ye not much better than they?
²⁷ Which of you by taking thought can add one cubit unto his stature?
²⁸ And why take ye thought for raiment? Consider the lilies of the field, how they grow; they toil not, neither do they spin:
²⁹ And yet I say unto you, That even Solomon in all his glory was not arrayed like one of these.
³⁰ Wherefore, if God so clothe the grass of the field, which to day is, and to morrow is cast into the oven, shall he not much more clothe you, O ye of little faith?
³¹ Therefore take no thought, saying, What shall we eat? or, What shall we drink? or, Wherewithal shall we be clothed?
³² (For after all these things do the Gentiles seek:) for your heavenly Father knoweth that ye have need of all these things.
³³ But seek ye first the kingdom of God, and his righteousness; and all these things shall be added unto you.
³⁴ Take therefore no thought for the morrow: for the morrow shall take thought for the things of itself. Sufficient unto the day is the evil thereof.

Oh! To be Like the Master

John 8:12, 28-29, 31 (KJV)

John 8:12 (KJV)
12 Then spake Jesus again unto them, saying, I am the light of the world: he that followeth me shall not walk in darkness, but shall have the light of life.

John 8:28-29 (KJV)
28 Then said Jesus unto them, When ye have lifted up the Son of man, then shall ye know that I am he, and that I do nothing of myself; but as my Father hath taught me, I speak these things.
29 And he that sent me is with me: the Father hath not left me alone; for I do always those things that please him.

John 8:31 (KJV)
31 Then said Jesus to those Jews which believed on him, If ye continue in my word, then are ye my disciples indeed;

Dr. Lydia A. Woods

Somethin' Told Me

John 12:26; Ephesians 4:30; Luke 2:26 (KJV)

John 12:26 (KJV)
26 If any man serve me, let him follow me; and where I am, there shall also my servant be: if any man serve me, him will my Father honour.

Ephesians 4:30 (KJV)
30 And grieve not the holy Spirit of God, whereby ye are sealed unto the day of redemption.

Luke 2:26 (KJV)
26 And it was revealed unto him by the Holy Ghost, that he should not see death, before he had seen the Lord's Christ.

Acceptance with Joy

Take a Visit to the Upper Room

Acts 1:3-4, 8, 2:1-21 (KJV)

Acts 1:3-4 (KJV)
3 To whom also he shewed himself alive after his passion by many infallible proofs, being seen of them forty days, and speaking of the things pertaining to the kingdom of God:
4 And, being assembled together with them, commanded them that they should not depart from Jerusalem, but wait for the promise of the Father, which, saith he, ye have heard of me.

Acts 1:8 (KJV)
8 But ye shall receive power, after that the Holy Ghost is come upon you: and ye shall be witnesses unto me both in Jerusalem, and in all Judaea, and in Samaria, and unto the uttermost part of the earth.

Acts 2:1-21 (KJV)
1 And when the day of Pentecost was fully come, they were all with one accord in one place.
2 And suddenly there came a sound from heaven as of a rushing mighty wind, and it filled all the house where they were sitting.
3 And there appeared unto them cloven tongues like as of fire, and it sat upon each of them.
4 And they were all filled with the Holy Ghost, and began to speak with other tongues, as the Spirit gave them utterance.
5 And there were dwelling at Jerusalem Jews, devout men, out of every nation under heaven.
6 Now when this was noised abroad, the multitude came together, and were confounded, because that every man heard them speak in his own language.
7 And they were all amazed and marvelled, saying one to another, Behold, are not all these which speak Galilaeans?

⁸ And how hear we every man in our own tongue, wherein we were born?
⁹ Parthians, and Medes, and Elamites, and the dwellers in Mesopotamia, and in Judaea, and Cappadocia, in Pontus, and Asia,
¹⁰ Phrygia, and Pamphylia, in Egypt, and in the parts of Libya about Cyrene, and strangers of Rome, Jews and proselytes,
¹¹ Cretes and Arabians, we do hear them speak in our tongues the wonderful works of God.
¹² And they were all amazed, and were in doubt, saying one to another, What meaneth this?
¹³ Others mocking said, These men are full of new wine.
¹⁴ But Peter, standing up with the eleven, lifted up his voice, and said unto them, Ye men of Judaea, and all ye that dwell at Jerusalem, be this known unto you, and hearken to my words:
¹⁵ For these are not drunken, as ye suppose, seeing it is but the third hour of the day.
¹⁶ But this is that which was spoken by the prophet Joel;
¹⁷ And it shall come to pass in the last days, saith God, I will pour out of my Spirit upon all flesh: and your sons and your daughters shall prophesy, and your young men shall see visions, and your old men shall dream dreams:
¹⁸ And on my servants and on my handmaidens I will pour out in those days of my Spirit; and they shall prophesy:
¹⁹ And I will shew wonders in heaven above, and signs in the earth beneath; blood, and fire, and vapour of smoke:
²⁰ The sun shall be turned into darkness, and the moon into blood, before the great and notable day of the Lord come:
²¹ And it shall come to pass, that whosoever shall call on the name of the Lord shall be saved.

The Time is Short!

Mark 13:20; Acts 1:7; I Thessalonians 5:1-2; II Peter 3 (KJV)

Mark 13:20 (KJV)
20 And except that the Lord had shortened those days, no flesh should be saved: but for the elect's sake, whom he hath chosen, he hath shortened the days.

Acts 1:7 (KJV)
7 And he said unto them, It is not for you to know the times or the seasons, which the Father hath put in his own power.

I Thessalonians 5:1-2 (KJV)
1 But of the times and the seasons, brethren, ye have no need that I write unto you.
2 For yourselves know perfectly that the day of the Lord so cometh as a thief in the night.

II Peter 3 (KJV)
1 This second epistle, beloved, I now write unto you; in both which I stir up your pure minds by way of remembrance:
2 That ye may be mindful of the words which were spoken before by the holy prophets, and of the commandment of us the apostles of the Lord and Saviour:
3 Knowing this first, that there shall come in the last days scoffers, walking after their own lusts,
4 And saying, Where is the promise of his coming? for since the fathers fell asleep, all things continue as they were from the beginning of the creation.
5 For this they willingly are ignorant of, that by the word of God the heavens were of old, and the earth standing out of the water and in the water:

⁶ Whereby the world that then was, being overflowed with water, perished:
⁷ But the heavens and the earth, which are now, by the same word are kept in store, reserved unto fire against the day of judgment and perdition of ungodly men.
⁸ But, beloved, be not ignorant of this one thing, that one day is with the Lord as a thousand years, and a thousand years as one day.
⁹ The Lord is not slack concerning his promise, as some men count slackness; but is longsuffering to us-ward, not willing that any should perish, but that all should come to repentance.
¹⁰ But the day of the Lord will come as a thief in the night; in the which the heavens shall pass away with a great noise, and the elements shall melt with fervent heat, the earth also and the works that are therein shall be burned up.
¹¹ Seeing then that all these things shall be dissolved, what manner of persons ought ye to be in all holy conversation and godliness,
¹² Looking for and hasting unto the coming of the day of God, wherein the heavens being on fire shall be dissolved, and the elements shall melt with fervent heat?
¹³ Nevertheless we, according to his promise, look for new heavens and a new earth, wherein dwelleth righteousness.
¹⁴ Wherefore, beloved, seeing that ye look for such things, be diligent that ye may be found of him in peace, without spot, and blameless.
¹⁵ And account that the longsuffering of our Lord is salvation; even as our beloved brother Paul also according to the wisdom given unto him hath written unto you;

Acceptance with Joy

¹⁶ As also in all his epistles, speaking in them of these things; in which are some things hard to be understood, which they that are unlearned and unstable wrest, as they do also the other scriptures, unto their own destruction.

¹⁷ Ye therefore, beloved, seeing ye know these things before, beware lest ye also, being led away with the error of the wicked, fall from your own stedfastness.

¹⁸ But grow in grace, and in the knowledge of our Lord and Saviour Jesus Christ. To him be glory both now and for ever. Amen.

Dr. Lydia A. Woods

Was He Saved? Did He Know the Lord?

John 13:34-35; I John 4:21 (KJV)

John 13:34-35 (KJV)
34 A new commandment I give unto you, That ye love one another; as I have loved you, that ye also love one another.
35 By this shall all men know that ye are my disciples, if ye have love one to another.

I John 4:21 (KJV)
21 And this commandment have we from him, That he who loveth God love his brother also.

Food for Saints

Dr. Lydia A. Woods

Above All

John 14:13; I John 5:14; Ephesians 3:10 (KJV)

John 14:13 (KJV)
¹³ And whatsoever ye shall ask in my name, that will I do, that the Father may be glorified in the Son.

I John 5:14 (KJV)
¹⁴ And this is the confidence that we have in him, that, if we ask any thing according to his will, he heareth us:

Ephesians 3:10 (KJV)
¹⁰ To the intent that now unto the principalities and powers in heavenly places might be known by the church the manifold wisdom of God,

Be Still!

Psalm 46:10 (KJV)

Psalm 46:10 (KJV)
[10] Be still, and know that I am God: I will be exalted among the heathen, I will be exalted in the earth.

Dr. Lydia A. Woods

Children of the King

I John 3:1, 9; Psalm 91:11; Matthew 4:6 (KJV)

I John 3:1 (KJV)
¹ Behold, what manner of love the Father hath bestowed upon us, that we should be called the sons of God: therefore the world knoweth us not, because it knew him not.

I John 3:9 (KJV)
⁹ Whosoever is born of God doth not commit sin; for his seed remaineth in him: and he cannot sin, because he is born of God.

Psalm 91:11 (KJV)
¹¹ For he shall give his angels charge over thee, to keep thee in all thy ways.

Matthew 4:6 (KJV)
⁶ And saith unto him, If thou be the Son of God, cast thyself down: for it is written, He shall give his angels charge concerning thee: and in their hands they shall bear thee up, lest at any time thou dash thy foot against a stone.

Doin' the Adam

Genesis 3:1-24 (KJV)

Genesis 3:1-24 (KJV)
1 Now the serpent was more subtil than any beast of the field which the LORD God had made. And he said unto the woman, Yea, hath God said, Ye shall not eat of every tree of the garden?
2 And the woman said unto the serpent, We may eat of the fruit of the trees of the garden:
3 But of the fruit of the tree which is in the midst of the garden, God hath said, Ye shall not eat of it, neither shall ye touch it, lest ye die.
4 And the serpent said unto the woman, Ye shall not surely die:
5 For God doth know that in the day ye eat thereof, then your eyes shall be opened, and ye shall be as gods, knowing good and evil.
6 And when the woman saw that the tree was good for food, and that it was pleasant to the eyes, and a tree to be desired to make one wise, she took of the fruit thereof, and did eat, and gave also unto her husband with her; and he did eat.
7 And the eyes of them both were opened, and they knew that they were naked; and they sewed fig leaves together, and made themselves aprons.
8 And they heard the voice of the LORD God walking in the garden in the cool of the day: and Adam and his wife hid themselves from the presence of the LORD God amongst the trees of the garden.
9 And the LORD God called unto Adam, and said unto him, Where art thou?
10 And he said, I heard thy voice in the garden, and I was afraid, because I was naked; and I hid myself.
11 And he said, Who told thee that thou wast naked? Hast thou eaten of the tree, whereof I commanded thee that thou shouldest not eat?

Dr. Lydia A. Woods

¹² And the man said, The woman whom thou gavest to be with me, she gave me of the tree, and I did eat.
¹³ And the LORD God said unto the woman, What is this that thou hast done? And the woman said, The serpent beguiled me, and I did eat.
¹⁴ And the LORD God said unto the serpent, Because thou hast done this, thou art cursed above all cattle, and above every beast of the field; upon thy belly shalt thou go, and dust shalt thou eat all the days of thy life:
¹⁵ And I will put enmity between thee and the woman, and between thy seed and her seed; it shall bruise thy head, and thou shalt bruise his heel.
¹⁶ Unto the woman he said, I will greatly multiply thy sorrow and thy conception; in sorrow thou shalt bring forth children; and thy desire shall be to thy husband, and he shall rule over thee.
¹⁷ And unto Adam he said, Because thou hast hearkened unto the voice of thy wife, and hast eaten of the tree, of which I commanded thee, saying, Thou shalt not eat of it: cursed is the ground for thy sake; in sorrow shalt thou eat of it all the days of thy life;
¹⁸ Thorns also and thistles shall it bring forth to thee; and thou shalt eat the herb of the field;
¹⁹ In the sweat of thy face shalt thou eat bread, till thou return unto the ground; for out of it wast thou taken: for dust thou art, and unto dust shalt thou return.
²⁰ And Adam called his wife's name Eve; because she was the mother of all living.
²¹ Unto Adam also and to his wife did the LORD God make coats of skins, and clothed them.

²² And the LORD God said, Behold, the man is become as one of us, to know good and evil: and now, lest he put forth his hand, and take also of the tree of life, and eat, and live for ever:
²³ Therefore the LORD God sent him forth from the garden of Eden, to till the ground from whence he was taken.
²⁴ So he drove out the man; and he placed at the east of the garden of Eden Cherubims, and a flaming sword which turned every way, to keep the way of the tree of life.

Dr. Lydia A. Woods

Father Knows Best

Proverbs 1:7; James 1:5 (KJV)

Proverbs 1:7 (KJV)
⁷ The fear of the LORD is the beginning of knowledge: but fools despise wisdom and instruction.

James 1:5 (KJV)
⁵ If any of you lack wisdom, let him ask of God, that giveth to all men liberally, and upbraideth not; and it shall be given him.

For the Elect's Sake

Mark 13:20 (KJV)

Mark 13:20 (KJV)
[20] And except that the Lord had shortened those days, no flesh should be saved: but for the elect's sake, whom he hath chosen, he hath shortened the days.

Dr. Lydia A. Woods

Get in the House

Exodus 12:12-14; James 2:12, 18-19 (KJV)

Exodus 12:12-14 (KJV)
¹² For I will pass through the land of Egypt this night, and will smite all the firstborn in the land of Egypt, both man and beast; and against all the gods of Egypt I will execute judgment: I am the LORD. ¹³ And the blood shall be to you for a token upon the houses where ye are: and when I see the blood, I will pass over you, and the plague shall not be upon you to destroy you, when I smite the land of Egypt. ¹⁴ And this day shall be unto you for a memorial; and ye shall keep it a feast to the LORD throughout your generations; ye shall keep it a feast by an ordinance for ever.

James 2:12 (KJV)
¹² So speak ye, and so do, as they that shall be judged by the law of liberty.

James 2:18-19 (KJV)
¹⁸ Yea, a man may say, Thou hast faith, and I have works: shew me thy faith without thy works, and I will shew thee my faith by my works. ¹⁹ Thou believest that there is one God; thou doest well: the devils also believe, and tremble.

Acceptance with Joy

God's M.O.

I Corinthians 1:26-27, 2:7, 3:19; Luke 2:7; Ephesians 3:5 (KJV)

I Corinthians 1:26-27 (KJV)
26 For ye see your calling, brethren, how that not many wise men after the flesh, not many mighty, not many noble, are called:
27 But God hath chosen the foolish things of the world to confound the wise; and God hath chosen the weak things of the world to confound the things which are mighty;

I Corinthians 2:7 (KJV)
7 But we speak the wisdom of God in a mystery, even the hidden wisdom, which God ordained before the world unto our glory:

I Corinthians 3:19 (KJV)
19 For the wisdom of this world is foolishness with God. For it is written, He taketh the wise in their own craftiness.

Luke 2:7 (KJV)
7 And she brought forth her firstborn son, and wrapped him in swaddling clothes, and laid him in a manger; because there was no room for them in the inn.

Ephesians 3:5 (KJV)
5 Which in other ages was not made known unto the sons of men, as it is now revealed unto his holy apostles and prophets by the Spirit;

Dr. Lydia A. Woods

I'm Not Lucky - I'm Blessed!

Genesis 12:3, 26:4; Deuteronomy 7:3-14 (KJV)

Genesis 12:3 (KJV)
3 And I will bless them that bless thee, and curse him that curseth thee: and in thee shall all families of the earth be blessed.

Genesis 26:4 (KJV)
4 And I will make thy seed to multiply as the stars of heaven, and will give unto thy seed all these countries; and in thy seed shall all the nations of the earth be blessed;

Deuteronomy 7:3-14 (KJV)
3 Neither shalt thou make marriages with them; thy daughter thou shalt not give unto his son, nor his daughter shalt thou take unto thy son.
4 For they will turn away thy son from following me, that they may serve other gods: so will the anger of the LORD be kindled against you, and destroy thee suddenly.
5 But thus shall ye deal with them; ye shall destroy their altars, and break down their images, and cut down their groves, and burn their graven images with fire.
6 For thou art an holy people unto the LORD thy God: the LORD thy God hath chosen thee to be a special people unto himself, above all people that are upon the face of the earth.
7 The LORD did not set his love upon you, nor choose you, because ye were more in number than any people; for ye were the fewest of all people:
8 But because the LORD loved you, and because he would keep the oath which he had sworn unto your fathers, hath the LORD brought you out with a mighty hand, and redeemed you out of the house of bondmen, from the hand of Pharaoh king of Egypt.

Acceptance with Joy

⁹ Know therefore that the LORD thy God, he is God, the faithful God, which keepeth covenant and mercy with them that love him and keep his commandments to a thousand generations;

¹⁰ And repayeth them that hate him to their face, to destroy them: he will not be slack to him that hateth him, he will repay him to his face.

¹¹ Thou shalt therefore keep the commandments, and the statutes, and the judgments, which I command thee this day, to do them.

¹² Wherefore it shall come to pass, if ye hearken to these judgments, and keep, and do them, that the LORD thy God shall keep unto thee the covenant and the mercy which he sware unto thy fathers:

¹³ And he will love thee, and bless thee, and multiply thee: he will also bless the fruit of thy womb, and the fruit of thy land, thy corn, and thy wine, and thine oil, the increase of thy kine, and the flocks of thy sheep, in the land which he sware unto thy fathers to give thee.

¹⁴ Thou shalt be blessed above all people: there shall not be male or female barren among you, or among your cattle.

Dr. Lydia A. Woods

I'm Tired!

John 16:33; Ephesians 5:3-5 (KJV)

John 16:33 (KJV)
33 These things I have spoken unto you, that in me ye might have peace. In the world ye shall have tribulation: but be of good cheer; I have overcome the world.

Ephesians 5:3-5 (KJV)
3 But fornication, and all uncleanness, or covetousness, let it not be once named among you, as becometh saints;
4 Neither filthiness, nor foolish talking, nor jesting, which are not convenient: but rather giving of thanks.
5 For this ye know, that no whoremonger, nor unclean person, nor covetous man, who is an idolater, hath any inheritance in the kingdom of Christ and of God.

If You Loved Me Lord...

Romans 8:26; James 4:3 (KJV)

Romans 8:26 (KJV)
26 Likewise the Spirit also helpeth our infirmities: for we know not what we should pray for as we ought: but the Spirit itself maketh intercession for us with groanings which cannot be uttered.

James 4:3 (KJV)
3 Ye ask, and receive not, because ye ask amiss, that ye may consume it upon your lusts.

Dr. Lydia A. Woods

It's Alright

James 1:5 (KJV)

James 1:5 (KJV)
⁵ If any of you lack wisdom, let him ask of God, that giveth to all men liberally, and upbraideth not; and it shall be given him.

Just Wait!

Psalm 25:3, 27:14, 37:18; Isaiah 40:31 (KJV)

Psalm 25:3 (KJV)
³ Yea, let none that wait on thee be ashamed: let them be ashamed which transgress without cause.

Psalm 27:14 (KJV)
¹⁴ Wait on the LORD: be of good courage, and he shall strengthen thine heart: wait, I say, on the LORD.

Psalm 37:18 (KJV)
¹⁸ The LORD knoweth the days of the upright: and their inheritance shall be for ever.

Isaiah 40:31 (KJV)
³¹ But they that wait upon the LORD shall renew their strength; they shall mount up with wings as eagles; they shall run, and not be weary; and they shall walk, and not faint.

Dr. Lydia A. Woods

Know Your Enemy

Matthew 4:1-11; Mark 16:17 (KJV)

Matthew 4:1-11 Version (KJV)
[1] Then was Jesus led up of the Spirit into the wilderness to be tempted of the devil.
[2] And when he had fasted forty days and forty nights, he was afterward an hungred.
[3] And when the tempter came to him, he said, If thou be the Son of God, command that these stones be made bread.
[4] But he answered and said, It is written, Man shall not live by bread alone, but by every word that proceedeth out of the mouth of God.
[5] Then the devil taketh him up into the holy city, and setteth him on a pinnacle of the temple,
[6] And saith unto him, If thou be the Son of God, cast thyself down: for it is written, He shall give his angels charge concerning thee: and in their hands they shall bear thee up, lest at any time thou dash thy foot against a stone.
[7] Jesus said unto him, It is written again, Thou shalt not tempt the Lord thy God.
[8] Again, the devil taketh him up into an exceeding high mountain, and sheweth him all the kingdoms of the world, and the glory of them;
[9] And saith unto him, All these things will I give thee, if thou wilt fall down and worship me.
[10] Then saith Jesus unto him, Get thee hence, Satan: for it is written, Thou shalt worship the Lord thy God, and him only shalt thou serve.
[11] Then the devil leaveth him, and, behold, angels came and ministered unto him.

Acceptance with Joy

Mark 16:17 (KJV)
[17] And these signs shall follow them that believe; In my name shall they cast out devils; they shall speak with new tongues;

Lean Not

Proverbs 3:5-6; James 1:5 (KJV)

Proverbs 3:5-6 (KJV)
[5] Trust in the LORD with all thine heart; and lean not unto thine own understanding.
[6] In all thy ways acknowledge him, and he shall direct thy paths.

James 1:5 (KJV)
[5] If any of you lack wisdom, let him ask of God, that giveth to all men liberally, and upbraideth not; and it shall be given him.

Love is an Action

Philippians 4:19 (KJV)

Philippians 4:19 (KJV)
[19] But my God shall supply all your need according to his riches in glory by Christ Jesus.

Dr. Lydia A. Woods

So What's-Up With That!

Malachi 3:13-17 (KJV)

Malachi 3:13-17 (KJV)
[13] Your words have been stout against me, saith the LORD. Yet ye say, What have we spoken so much against thee?
[14] Ye have said, It is vain to serve God: and what profit is it that we have kept his ordinance, and that we have walked mournfully before the LORD of hosts?
[15] And now we call the proud happy; yea, they that work wickedness are set up; yea, they that tempt God are even delivered.
[16] Then they that feared the LORD spake often one to another: and the LORD hearkened, and heard it, and a book of remembrance was written before him for them that feared the LORD, and that thought upon his name.
[17] And they shall be mine, saith the LORD of hosts, in that day when I make up my jewels; and I will spare them, as a man spareth his own son that serveth him.

Take Out the Trash!

Ephesians 6:18; James 5:13; I Thessalonians 5:17; Romans 8:16 (KJV)

Ephesians 6:18 (KJV)
18 Praying always with all prayer and supplication in the Spirit, and watching thereunto with all perseverance and supplication for all saints;

James 5:13 (KJV)
13 Is any among you afflicted? let him pray. Is any merry? let him sing psalms.

I Thessalonians 5:17 (KJV)
17 Pray without ceasing.

Romans 8:16 (KJV)
16 The Spirit itself beareth witness with our spirit, that we are the children of God:

Dr. Lydia A. Woods

Unable to Receive

Luke 6:38; Malachi 3:10 (KJV)

Luke 6:38 (KJV)
38 Give, and it shall be given unto you; good measure, pressed down, and shaken together, and running over, shall men give into your bosom. For with the same measure that ye mete withal it shall be measured to you again.

Malachi 3:10 (KJV)
10 Bring ye all the tithes into the storehouse, that there may be meat in mine house, and prove me now herewith, saith the LORD of hosts, if I will not open you the windows of heaven, and pour you out a blessing, that there shall not be room enough to receive it.

With Persecution...

Matthew 5:10-12; II Corinthians 4:9-18 (KJV)

Matthew 5:10-12 (KJV)
¹⁰ Blessed are they which are persecuted for righteousness' sake: for theirs is the kingdom of heaven.
¹¹ Blessed are ye, when men shall revile you, and persecute you, and shall say all manner of evil against you falsely, for my sake.
¹² Rejoice, and be exceeding glad: for great is your reward in heaven: for so persecuted they the prophets which were before you.

II Corinthians 4:9-18 (KJV)
⁹ Persecuted, but not forsaken; cast down, but not destroyed;
¹⁰ Always bearing about in the body the dying of the Lord Jesus, that the life also of Jesus might be made manifest in our body.
¹¹ For we which live are always delivered unto death for Jesus' sake, that the life also of Jesus might be made manifest in our mortal flesh.
¹² So then death worketh in us, but life in you.
¹³ We having the same spirit of faith, according as it is written, I believed, and therefore have I spoken; we also believe, and therefore speak;
¹⁴ Knowing that he which raised up the Lord Jesus shall raise up us also by Jesus, and shall present us with you.
¹⁵ For all things are for your sakes, that the abundant grace might through the thanksgiving of many redound to the glory of God.
¹⁶ For which cause we faint not; but though our outward man perish, yet the inward man is renewed day by day.
¹⁷ For our light affliction, which is but for a moment, worketh for us a far more exceeding and eternal weight of glory;

Dr. Lydia A. Woods

18 While we look not at the things which are seen, but at the things which are not seen: for the things which are seen are temporal; but the things which are not seen are eternal.

Let Those With Ears...

Dr. Lydia A. Woods

Answer to Many a Prayer

John 16:33; Romans 5:3, 12:12 (KJV)

John 16:33 (KJV)
33 These things I have spoken unto you, that in me ye might have peace. In the world ye shall have tribulation: but be of good cheer; I have overcome the world.

Romans 5:3 (KJV)
3 And not only so, but we glory in tribulations also: knowing that tribulation worketh patience;

Romans 12:12 (KJV)
12 Rejoicing in hope; patient in tribulation; continuing instant in prayer;

Blood Disguise

Ephesians 1:7; Acts 20:28; Hebrews 9:22 (KJV)

Ephesians 1:7 (KJV)
7 In whom we have redemption through his blood, the forgiveness of sins, according to the riches of his grace;

Acts 20:28 (KJV)
28 Take heed therefore unto yourselves, and to all the flock, over the which the Holy Ghost hath made you overseers, to feed the church of God, which he hath purchased with his own blood.

Dr. Lydia A. Woods

Boys Into Men

Isaiah 54:13; Hebrews 12:6; Revelation 3:19 (KJV)

Isaiah 54:13 (KJV)
13 And all thy children shall be taught of the LORD; and great shall be the peace of thy children.

Hebrews 12:6 (KJV)
6 For whom the Lord loveth he chasteneth, and scourgeth every son whom he receiveth.

Revelation 3:19 (KJV)
19 As many as I love, I rebuke and chasten: be zealous therefore, and repent.

The Building You Call Church

Colossians 1:18; Matthew 16:18; Ephesians 5:27 (KJV)

Colossians 1:18 (KJV)
18 And he is the head of the body, the church: who is the beginning, the firstborn from the dead; that in all things he might have the preeminence.

Matthew 16:18 (KJV)
18 And I say also unto thee, That thou art Peter, and upon this rock I will build my church; and the gates of hell shall not prevail against it.

Ephesians 5:27 (KJV)
27 That he might present it to himself a glorious church, not having spot, or wrinkle, or any such thing; but that it should be holy and without blemish.

Dr. Lydia A. Woods

Don't Forsake the Assembly

Hebrews 10:25; Matthew 18:20 (KJV)

Hebrews 10:25 (KJV)
[25] Not forsaking the assembling of ourselves together, as the manner of some is; but exhorting one another: and so much the more, as ye see the day approaching.

Matthew 18:20 (KJV)
[20] For where two or three are gathered together in my name, there am I in the midst of them.

E.T.

(E.T, the Movie) John 14:1-4 (KJV)

John 14:1-4 (KJV)
¹ Let not your heart be troubled: ye believe in God, believe also in me.
² In my Father's house are many mansions: if it were not so, I would have told you. I go to prepare a place for you.
³ And if I go and prepare a place for you, I will come again, and receive you unto myself; that where I am, there ye may be also.
⁴ And whither I go ye know, and the way ye know.

Dr. Lydia A. Woods

Fruit Trees

Galatians 5:22-23 (KJV)

Galatians 5:22-23 (KJV)
[22] But the fruit of the Spirit is love, joy, peace, longsuffering, gentleness, goodness, faith,
[23] Meekness, temperance: against such there is no law.

Generations in You

Psalm 127:3-5, 128:3 (KJV)

Psalm 127:3-5 (KJV)
³ Lo, children are an heritage of the LORD: and the fruit of the womb is his reward.
⁴ As arrows are in the hand of a mighty man; so are children of the youth.
⁵ Happy is the man that hath his quiver full of them: they shall not be ashamed, but they shall speak with the enemies in the gate.

Psalm 128:3 (KJV)
³ Thy wife shall be as a fruitful vine by the sides of thine house: thy children like olive plants round about thy table.

Dr. Lydia A. Woods

The Gift

Psalm 111:10; Proverbs 16:16-25 (KJV)

Psalm 111:10 (KJV)
[10] The fear of the LORD is the beginning of wisdom: a good understanding have all they that do his commandments: his praise endureth for ever.

Proverbs 16:16-25 (KJV)
[16] How much better is it to get wisdom than gold! and to get understanding rather to be chosen than silver!
[17] The highway of the upright is to depart from evil: he that keepeth his way preserveth his soul.
[18] Pride goeth before destruction, and an haughty spirit before a fall.
[19] Better it is to be of an humble spirit with the lowly, than to divide the spoil with the proud.
[20] He that handleth a matter wisely shall find good: and whoso trusteth in the LORD, happy is he.
[21] The wise in heart shall be called prudent: and the sweetness of the lips increaseth learning.
[22] Understanding is a wellspring of life unto him that hath it: but the instruction of fools is folly.
[23] The heart of the wise teacheth his mouth, and addeth learning to his lips.
[24] Pleasant words are as an honeycomb, sweet to the soul, and health to the bones.
[25] There is a way that seemeth right unto a man, but the end thereof are the ways of death.

Has Done, Is Doing or Will Do

Psalm 71:15, 35:28, 40:5; Job 9:10 (KJV)

Psalm 71:15 (KJV)
15 My mouth shall shew forth thy righteousness and thy salvation all the day; for I know not the numbers thereof.

Psalm 35:28 (KJV)
28 And my tongue shall speak of thy righteousness and of thy praise all the day long.

Psalm 40:5 (KJV)
5 Many, O LORD my God, are thy wonderful works which thou hast done, and thy thoughts which are to us-ward: they cannot be reckoned up in order unto thee: if I would declare and speak of them, they are more than can be numbered.

Job 9:10 (KJV)
10 Which doeth great things past finding out; yea, and wonders without number.

Dr. Lydia A. Woods

Holy Rollers

I Peter 1:23, 2:9; John 1:12-13; I John 5:1 (KJV)

I Peter 1:23 (KJV)
[23] Being born again, not of corruptible seed, but of incorruptible, by the word of God, which liveth and abideth for ever.

I Peter 2:9 (KJV)
[9] But ye are a chosen generation, a royal priesthood, an holy nation, a peculiar people; that ye should shew forth the praises of him who hath called you out of darkness into his marvellous light;

John 1:12-13 (KJV)
[12] But as many as received him, to them gave he power to become the sons of God, even to them that believe on his name:
[13] Which were born, not of blood, nor of the will of the flesh, nor of the will of man, but of God.

I John 5:1 (KJV)
[1] Whosoever believeth that Jesus is the Christ is born of God: and every one that loveth him that begat loveth him also that is begotten of him.

Jesus Learned Obedience

Hebrews 5:8 (KJV)

Hebrews 5:8 (KJV)
8 Though he were a Son, yet learned he obedience by the things which he suffered;

Dr. Lydia A. Woods

Just Give It!

Acts 20:35; Luke 6:34-38 (KJV)

Acts 20:35 (KJV)
35 I have shewed you all things, how that so labouring ye ought to support the weak, and to remember the words of the Lord Jesus, how he said, It is more blessed to give than to receive.

Luke 6:34-38 (KJV)
34 And if ye lend to them of whom ye hope to receive, what thank have ye? for sinners also lend to sinners, to receive as much again.
35 But love ye your enemies, and do good, and lend, hoping for nothing again; and your reward shall be great, and ye shall be the children of the Highest: for he is kind unto the unthankful and to the evil.
36 Be ye therefore merciful, as your Father also is merciful.
37 Judge not, and ye shall not be judged: condemn not, and ye shall not be condemned: forgive, and ye shall be forgiven:
38 Give, and it shall be given unto you; good measure, pressed down, and shaken together, and running over, shall men give into your bosom. For with the same measure that ye mete withal it shall be measured to you again.

Liar, Liar

II Timothy 2:11; Romans 6:3-4 (KJV)

II Timothy 2:11 (KJV)
11 It is a faithful saying: For if we be dead with him, we shall also live with him:

Romans 6:3-4 (KJV)
3 Know ye not, that so many of us as were baptized into Jesus Christ were baptized into his death?
4 Therefore we are buried with him by baptism into death: that like as Christ was raised up from the dead by the glory of the Father, even so we also should walk in newness of life.

Dr. Lydia A. Woods

My God Isn't Stupid!

Genesis 2:8-9 (KJV)

Genesis 2:8-9 (KJV)
8 And the LORD God planted a garden eastward in Eden; and there he put the man whom he had formed.
9 And out of the ground made the LORD God to grow every tree that is pleasant to the sight, and good for food; the tree of life also in the midst of the garden, and the tree of knowledge of good and evil.

Not in a Place Called Church

II Peter 2:1-3; II Timothy 2:15; II Corinthians 6:16 (KJV)

II Peter 2:1-3 (KJV)
[1] But there were false prophets also among the people, even as there shall be false teachers among you, who privily shall bring in damnable heresies, even denying the Lord that bought them, and bring upon themselves swift destruction.
[2] And many shall follow their pernicious ways; by reason of whom the way of truth shall be evil spoken of.
[3] And through covetousness shall they with feigned words make merchandise of you: whose judgment now of a long time lingereth not, and their damnation slumbereth not.

II Timothy 2:15 (KJV)
[15] Study to shew thyself approved unto God, a workman that needeth not to be ashamed, rightly dividing the word of truth.

II Corinthians 6:16 (KJV)
[16] And what agreement hath the temple of God with idols? for ye are the temple of the living God; as God hath said, I will dwell in them, and walk in them; and I will be their God, and they shall be my people.

Dr. Lydia A. Woods

Obedience the Highest Form of Praise

Hebrews 5:8; Romans 5:19; Philippians 2:8 (KJV)

Hebrews 5:8 (KJV)
8 Though he were a Son, yet learned he obedience by the things which he suffered;

Romans 5:19 (KJV)
19 For as by one man's disobedience many were made sinners, so by the obedience of one shall many be made righteous.

Philippians 2:8 (KJV)
8 And being found in fashion as a man, he humbled himself, and became obedient unto death, even the death of the cross.

A Compilation of Christian Poetry *Let Those With Ears...*

The Perfect Murder

Romans 7:14-21 (KJV)

Romans 7:14-21 (KJV)
14 For we know that the law is spiritual: but I am carnal, sold under sin.
15 For that which I do I allow not: for what I would, that do I not; but what I hate, that do I.
16 If then I do that which I would not, I consent unto the law that it is good.
17 Now then it is no more I that do it, but sin that dwelleth in me.
18 For I know that in me (that is, in my flesh,) dwelleth no good thing: for to will is present with me; but how to perform that which is good I find not.
19 For the good that I would I do not: but the evil which I would not, that I do.
20 Now if I do that I would not, it is no more I that do it, but sin that dwelleth in me.
21 I find then a law, that, when I would do good, evil is present with me.

Resistance is Futile

I Corinthians 6:17, 12:12-27 (KJV)

I Corinthians 6:17 (KJV)
17 But he that is joined unto the Lord is one spirit.

I Corinthians 12:12-27 (KJV)
12 For as the body is one, and hath many members, and all the members of that one body, being many, are one body: so also is Christ.

13 For by one Spirit are we all baptized into one body, whether we be Jews or Gentiles, whether we be bond or free; and have been all made to drink into one Spirit.

14 For the body is not one member, but many.

15 If the foot shall say, Because I am not the hand, I am not of the body; is it therefore not of the body?

16 And if the ear shall say, Because I am not the eye, I am not of the body; is it therefore not of the body?

17 If the whole body were an eye, where were the hearing? If the whole were hearing, where were the smelling?

18 But now hath God set the members every one of them in the body, as it hath pleased him.

19 And if they were all one member, where were the body?

20 But now are they many members, yet but one body.

21 And the eye cannot say unto the hand, I have no need of thee: nor again the head to the feet, I have no need of you.

22 Nay, much more those members of the body, which seem to be more feeble, are necessary:

23 And those members of the body, which we think to be less honourable, upon these we bestow more abundant honour; and our uncomely parts have more abundant comeliness.

Acceptance with Joy

[24] For our comely parts have no need: but God hath tempered the body together, having given more abundant honour to that part which lacked.
[25] That there should be no schism in the body; but that the members should have the same care one for another.
[26] And whether one member suffer, all the members suffer with it; or one member be honoured, all the members rejoice with it.
[27] Now ye are the body of Christ, and members in particular.

Dr. Lydia A. Woods

So Great a Cloud of Witnesses

Hebrews 12:1 (KJV)

Hebrews 12:1 (KJV)
[1] Wherefore seeing we also are compassed about with so great a cloud of witnesses, let us lay aside every weight, and the sin which doth so easily beset us, and let us run with patience the race that is set before us,

The U.P.S. Man

John 4:44; Psalm 105:15 (KJV)

John 4:44 (KJV)
44 For Jesus himself testified, that a prophet hath no honour in his own country.

Psalm 105:15 (KJV)
15 Saying, Touch not mine anointed, and do my prophets no harm.

Dr. Lydia A. Woods

Upside Down, Inside Out

Romans 1:21-32 (KJV)

Romans 1:21-32 (KJV)
21 Because that, when they knew God, they glorified him not as God, neither were thankful; but became vain in their imaginations, and their foolish heart was darkened.
22 Professing themselves to be wise, they became fools,
23 And changed the glory of the uncorruptible God into an image made like to corruptible man, and to birds, and fourfooted beasts, and creeping things.
24 Wherefore God also gave them up to uncleanness through the lusts of their own hearts, to dishonour their own bodies between themselves:
25 Who changed the truth of God into a lie, and worshipped and served the creature more than the Creator, who is blessed for ever. Amen.
26 For this cause God gave them up unto vile affections: for even their women did change the natural use into that which is against nature:
27 And likewise also the men, leaving the natural use of the woman, burned in their lust one toward another; men with men working that which is unseemly, and receiving in themselves that recompence of their error which was meet.
28 And even as they did not like to retain God in their knowledge, God gave them over to a reprobate mind, to do those things which are not convenient;
29 Being filled with all unrighteousness, fornication, wickedness, covetousness, maliciousness; full of envy, murder, debate, deceit, malignity; whisperers,
30 Backbiters, haters of God, despiteful, proud, boasters, inventors of evil things, disobedient to parents,

Acceptance with Joy

³¹ Without understanding, covenantbreakers, without natural affection, implacable, unmerciful:

³² Who knowing the judgment of God, that they which commit such things are worthy of death, not only do the same, but have pleasure in them that do them.

Dr. Lydia A. Woods

With His Own Blood

Acts 20:28; Hosea 2:19; Revelation 19:7-9, 21:9 (KJV)

Acts 20:28 (KJV)
28 Take heed therefore unto yourselves, and to all the flock, over the which the Holy Ghost hath made you overseers, to feed the church of God, which he hath purchased with his own blood.

Hosea 2:19 (KJV)
19 And I will betroth thee unto me for ever; yea, I will betroth thee unto me in righteousness, and in judgment, and in lovingkindness, and in mercies.

Revelation 19:7-9 (KJV)
7 Let us be glad and rejoice, and give honour to him: for the marriage of the Lamb is come, and his wife hath made herself ready.
8 And to her was granted that she should be arrayed in fine linen, clean and white: for the fine linen is the righteousness of saints.
9 And he saith unto me, Write, Blessed are they which are called unto the marriage supper of the Lamb. And he saith unto me, These are the true sayings of God.

Revelation 21:9 (KJV)
9 And there came unto me one of the seven angels which had the seven vials full of the seven last plagues, and talked with me, saying, Come hither, I will shew thee the bride, the Lamb's wife.

Conversations with the Saints

Dr. Lydia A. Woods

Ain't He All That!

Hebrews 1:2-3; John 1:1-5; Revelation 22:13 (KJV)

Hebrews 1:2-3 (KJV)
2 Hath in these last days spoken unto us by his Son, whom he hath appointed heir of all things, by whom also he made the worlds;
3 Who being the brightness of his glory, and the express image of his person, and upholding all things by the word of his power, when he had by himself purged our sins, sat down on the right hand of the Majesty on high:

John 1:1-5 (KJV)
1 In the beginning was the Word, and the Word was with God, and the Word was God.
2 The same was in the beginning with God.
3 All things were made by him; and without him was not any thing made that was made.
4 In him was life; and the life was the light of men.
5 And the light shineth in darkness; and the darkness comprehended it not.

Revelation 22:13 (KJV)
13 I am Alpha and Omega, the beginning and the end, the first and the last.

A Blessing – Not a Curse!

Psalm 127:3-5 (KJV)

Psalm 127:3-5 (KJV)
³ Lo, children are an heritage of the LORD: and the fruit of the womb is his reward.
⁴ As arrows are in the hand of a mighty man; so are children of the youth.
⁵ Happy is the man that hath his quiver full of them: they shall not be ashamed, but they shall speak with the enemies in the gate.

Dr. Lydia A. Woods

Call My Name

I Peter 2:9 (KJV)

I Peter 2:9 (KJV)
9 But ye are a chosen generation, a royal priesthood, an holy nation, a peculiar people; that ye should shew forth the praises of him who hath called you out of darkness into his marvellous light;

Cerebral Palsy

Philippians 1:6; I Thessalonians 5:24; I Corinthians 1:9 (KJV)

Philippians 1:6 (KJV)
6 Being confident of this very thing, that he which hath begun a good work in you will perform it until the day of Jesus Christ:

I Thessalonians 5:24 (KJV)
24 Faithful is he that calleth you, who also will do it.

I Corinthians 1:9 (KJV)
9 God is faithful, by whom ye were called unto the fellowship of his Son Jesus Christ our Lord.

Dr. Lydia A. Woods

Common Sense

I Corinthians 1:25, 3:19; II Corinthians 5:7; Proverbs 3:5-6 (KJV)

I Corinthians 1:25 (KJV)
25 Because the foolishness of God is wiser than men; and the weakness of God is stronger than men.

I Corinthians 3:19 (KJV)
19 For the wisdom of this world is foolishness with God. For it is written, He taketh the wise in their own craftiness.

II Corinthians 5:7 (KJV)
7 (For we walk by faith, not by sight:)

Proverbs 3:5-6 (KJV)
5 Trust in the LORD with all thine heart; and lean not unto thine own understanding.
6 In all thy ways acknowledge him, and he shall direct thy paths.

Convicted

Romans 7:14-25 (KJV)

Romans 7:14-25 (KJV)
[14] For we know that the law is spiritual: but I am carnal, sold under sin.
[15] For that which I do I allow not: for what I would, that do I not; but what I hate, that do I.
[16] If then I do that which I would not, I consent unto the law that it is good.
[17] Now then it is no more I that do it, but sin that dwelleth in me.
[18] For I know that in me (that is, in my flesh,) dwelleth no good thing: for to will is present with me; but how to perform that which is good I find not.
[19] For the good that I would I do not: but the evil which I would not, that I do.
[20] Now if I do that I would not, it is no more I that do it, but sin that dwelleth in me.
[21] I find then a law, that, when I would do good, evil is present with me.
[22] For I delight in the law of God after the inward man:
[23] But I see another law in my members, warring against the law of my mind, and bringing me into captivity to the law of sin which is in my members.
[24] O wretched man that I am! who shall deliver me from the body of this death?
[25] I thank God through Jesus Christ our Lord. So then with the mind I myself serve the law of God; but with the flesh the law of sin.

Denominations

Mark 3:24-25; I Corinthians 12:12-31 (KJV)

Mark 3:24-25 (KJV)
24 And if a kingdom be divided against itself, that kingdom cannot stand.
25 And if a house be divided against itself, that house cannot stand.

I Corinthians 12:12-31 (KJV)
12 For as the body is one, and hath many members, and all the members of that one body, being many, are one body: so also is Christ.
13 For by one Spirit are we all baptized into one body, whether we be Jews or Gentiles, whether we be bond or free; and have been all made to drink into one Spirit.
14 For the body is not one member, but many.
15 If the foot shall say, Because I am not the hand, I am not of the body; is it therefore not of the body?
16 And if the ear shall say, Because I am not the eye, I am not of the body; is it therefore not of the body?
17 If the whole body were an eye, where were the hearing? If the whole were hearing, where were the smelling?
18 But now hath God set the members every one of them in the body, as it hath pleased him.
19 And if they were all one member, where were the body?
20 But now are they many members, yet but one body.
21 And the eye cannot say unto the hand, I have no need of thee: nor again the head to the feet, I have no need of you.
22 Nay, much more those members of the body, which seem to be more feeble, are necessary:

Acceptance with Joy

²³ And those members of the body, which we think to be less honourable, upon these we bestow more abundant honour; and our uncomely parts have more abundant comeliness.

²⁴ For our comely parts have no need: but God hath tempered the body together, having given more abundant honour to that part which lacked.

²⁵ That there should be no schism in the body; but that the members should have the same care one for another.

²⁶ And whether one member suffer, all the members suffer with it; or one member be honoured, all the members rejoice with it.

²⁷ Now ye are the body of Christ, and members in particular.

²⁸ And God hath set some in the church, first apostles, secondarily prophets, thirdly teachers, after that miracles, then gifts of healings, helps, governments, diversities of tongues.

²⁹ Are all apostles? are all prophets? are all teachers? are all workers of miracles?

³⁰ Have all the gifts of healing? do all speak with tongues? do all interpret?

³¹ But covet earnestly the best gifts: and yet shew I unto you a more excellent way.

Dr. Lydia A. Woods

Forgive or Forgive Not

Luke 6:37; Mark 11:25-26 (KJV)

Luke 6:37 (KJV)
37 Judge not, and ye shall not be judged: condemn not, and ye shall not be condemned: forgive, and ye shall be forgiven:

Mark 11:25-26 (KJV)
25 And when ye stand praying, forgive, if ye have ought against any: that your Father also which is in heaven may forgive you your trespasses.
26 But if ye do not forgive, neither will your Father which is in heaven forgive your trespasses.

He's Good At...

Genesis 1:3, 9, 12, 16, 24, 27, 31; Isaiah 14:27, 46:9-11 (KJV)

Genesis 1:3 (KJV)
3 And God said, Let there be light: and there was light.

Genesis 1:9 (KJV)
9 And God said, Let the waters under the heaven be gathered together unto one place, and let the dry land appear: and it was so.

Genesis 1:12 (KJV)
12 And the earth brought forth grass, and herb yielding seed after his kind, and the tree yielding fruit, whose seed was in itself, after his kind: and God saw that it was good.

Genesis 1:16 (KJV)
16 And God made two great lights; the greater light to rule the day, and the lesser light to rule the night: he made the stars also.

Genesis 1:24 (KJV)
24 And God said, Let the earth bring forth the living creature after his kind, cattle, and creeping thing, and beast of the earth after his kind: and it was so.

Genesis 1:27 (KJV)
27 So God created man in his own image, in the image of God created he him; male and female created he them.

Genesis 1:31 (KJV)
31 And God saw every thing that he had made, and, behold, it was very good. And the evening and the morning were the sixth day.

Isaiah 14:27 (KJV)
27 For the LORD of hosts hath purposed, and who shall disannul it? and his hand is stretched out, and who shall turn it back?

Isaiah 46:9-11 (KJV)

⁹ Remember the former things of old: for I am God, and there is none else; I am God, and there is none like me,

¹⁰ Declaring the end from the beginning, and from ancient times the things that are not yet done, saying, My counsel shall stand, and I will do all my pleasure:

¹¹ Calling a ravenous bird from the east, the man that executeth my counsel from a far country: yea, I have spoken it, I will also bring it to pass; I have purposed it, I will also do it.

If Thou Be...

Matthew 4:6 (KJV)

Matthew 4:6 (KJV)
⁶ And saith unto him, If thou be the Son of God, cast thyself down: for it is written, He shall give his angels charge concerning thee: and in their hands they shall bear thee up, lest at any time thou dash thy foot against a stone.

Dr. Lydia A. Woods

If You Will Be Great

Matthew 20:26; I Peter 5:3 (KJV)

Matthew 20:26 (KJV)
26 But it shall not be so among you: but whosoever will be great among you, let him be your minister;

I Peter 5:3 (KJV)
3 Neither as being lords over God's heritage, but being examples to the flock.

Just a Family Feud

Genesis 12:2, 17:6, 18:18 (KJV)

Genesis 12:2 (KJV)
² And I will make of thee a great nation, and I will bless thee, and make thy name great; and thou shalt be a blessing:

Genesis 17:6 (KJV)
⁶ And I will make thee exceeding fruitful, and I will make nations of thee, and kings shall come out of thee.

Genesis 18:18 (KJV)
¹⁸ Seeing that Abraham shall surely become a great and mighty nation, and all the nations of the earth shall be blessed in him?

Dr. Lydia A. Woods

The Kingdom is Like Unto...

Matthew 4:23, 13:10-11, 13:31-33, 20:1-16, 24:14, 25:1-30 (KJV)

Matthew 4:23 (KJV)
23 And Jesus went about all Galilee, teaching in their synagogues, and preaching the gospel of the kingdom, and healing all manner of sickness and all manner of disease among the people.

Matthew 13:10-11 (KJV)
10 And the disciples came, and said unto him, Why speakest thou unto them in parables?
11 He answered and said unto them, Because it is given unto you to know the mysteries of the kingdom of heaven, but to them it is not given.

Matthew 13:31-33 (KJV)
31 Another parable put he forth unto them, saying, The kingdom of heaven is like to a grain of mustard seed, which a man took, and sowed in his field:
32 Which indeed is the least of all seeds: but when it is grown, it is the greatest among herbs, and becometh a tree, so that the birds of the air come and lodge in the branches thereof.
33 Another parable spake he unto them; The kingdom of heaven is like unto leaven, which a woman took, and hid in three measures of meal, till the whole was leavened.

Matthew 20:1-16 (KJV)
1 For the kingdom of heaven is like unto a man that is an householder, which went out early in the morning to hire labourers into his vineyard.
2 And when he had agreed with the labourers for a penny a day, he sent them into his vineyard.

Acceptance with Joy

³ And he went out about the third hour, and saw others standing idle in the marketplace,
⁴ And said unto them; Go ye also into the vineyard, and whatsoever is right I will give you. And they went their way.
⁵ Again he went out about the sixth and ninth hour, and did likewise.
⁶ And about the eleventh hour he went out, and found others standing idle, and saith unto them, Why stand ye here all the day idle?
⁷ They say unto him, Because no man hath hired us. He saith unto them, Go ye also into the vineyard; and whatsoever is right, that shall ye receive.
⁸ So when even was come, the lord of the vineyard saith unto his steward, Call the labourers, and give them their hire, beginning from the last unto the first.
⁹ And when they came that were hired about the eleventh hour, they received every man a penny.
¹⁰ But when the first came, they supposed that they should have received more; and they likewise received every man a penny.
¹¹ And when they had received it, they murmured against the goodman of the house,
¹² Saying, These last have wrought but one hour, and thou hast made them equal unto us, which have borne the burden and heat of the day.
¹³ But he answered one of them, and said, Friend, I do thee no wrong: didst not thou agree with me for a penny?
¹⁴ Take that thine is, and go thy way: I will give unto this last, even as unto thee.

¹⁵ Is it not lawful for me to do what I will with mine own? Is thine eye evil, because I am good?
¹⁶ So the last shall be first, and the first last: for many be called, but few chosen.

Matthew 24:14 (KJV)
¹⁴ And this gospel of the kingdom shall be preached in all the world for a witness unto all nations; and then shall the end come.

Matthew 25:1-30 (KJV)
¹ Then shall the kingdom of heaven be likened unto ten virgins, which took their lamps, and went forth to meet the bridegroom.
² And five of them were wise, and five were foolish.
³ They that were foolish took their lamps, and took no oil with them:
⁴ But the wise took oil in their vessels with their lamps.
⁵ While the bridegroom tarried, they all slumbered and slept.
⁶ And at midnight there was a cry made, Behold, the bridegroom cometh; go ye out to meet him.
⁷ Then all those virgins arose, and trimmed their lamps.
⁸ And the foolish said unto the wise, Give us of your oil; for our lamps are gone out.
⁹ But the wise answered, saying, Not so; lest there be not enough for us and you: but go ye rather to them that sell, and buy for yourselves.
¹⁰ And while they went to buy, the bridegroom came; and they that were ready went in with him to the marriage: and the door was shut.
¹¹ Afterward came also the other virgins, saying, Lord, Lord, open to us.
¹² But he answered and said, Verily I say unto you, I know you not.

Acceptance with Joy

[13] Watch therefore, for ye know neither the day nor the hour wherein the Son of man cometh.

[14] For the kingdom of heaven is as a man travelling into a far country, who called his own servants, and delivered unto them his goods.

[15] And unto one he gave five talents, to another two, and to another one; to every man according to his several ability; and straightway took his journey.

[16] Then he that had received the five talents went and traded with the same, and made them other five talents.

[17] And likewise he that had received two, he also gained other two.

[18] But he that had received one went and digged in the earth, and hid his lord's money.

[19] After a long time the lord of those servants cometh, and reckoneth with them.

[20] And so he that had received five talents came and brought other five talents, saying, Lord, thou deliveredst unto me five talents: behold, I have gained beside them five talents more.

[21] His lord said unto him, Well done, thou good and faithful servant: thou hast been faithful over a few things, I will make thee ruler over many things: enter thou into the joy of thy lord.

[22] He also that had received two talents came and said, Lord, thou deliveredst unto me two talents: behold, I have gained two other talents beside them.

[23] His lord said unto him, Well done, good and faithful servant; thou hast been faithful over a few things, I will make thee ruler over many things: enter thou into the joy of thy lord.

24 Then he which had received the one talent came and said, Lord, I knew thee that thou art an hard man, reaping where thou hast not sown, and gathering where thou hast not strawed:
25 And I was afraid, and went and hid thy talent in the earth: lo, there thou hast that is thine.
26 His lord answered and said unto him, Thou wicked and slothful servant, thou knewest that I reap where I sowed not, and gather where I have not strawed:
27 Thou oughtest therefore to have put my money to the exchangers, and then at my coming I should have received mine own with usury.
28 Take therefore the talent from him, and give it unto him which hath ten talents.
29 For unto every one that hath shall be given, and he shall have abundance: but from him that hath not shall be taken away even that which he hath.
30 And cast ye the unprofitable servant into outer darkness: there shall be weeping and gnashing of teeth.

Love You - Not Your Sin

Romans 1:26-27 (KJV)

Romans 1:26-27 (KJV)
[26] For this cause God gave them up unto vile affections: for even their women did change the natural use into that which is against nature:
[27] And likewise also the men, leaving the natural use of the woman, burned in their lust one toward another; men with men working that which is unseemly, and receiving in themselves that recompence of their error which was meet.

Dr. Lydia A. Woods

Only Human!

II Corinthians 5:17, 6:16 (KJV)

II Corinthians 5:17 (KJV)
[17] Therefore if any man be in Christ, he is a new creature: old things are passed away; behold, all things are become new.

II Corinthians 6:16 (KJV)
[16] And what agreement hath the temple of God with idols? for ye are the temple of the living God; as God hath said, I will dwell in them, and walk in them; and I will be their God, and they shall be my people.

Pro-Choice?

Mark 3:4; Exodus 20:13 (KJV)

Mark 3:4 (KJV)
4 And he saith unto them, Is it lawful to do good on the sabbath days, or to do evil? to save life, or to kill? But they held their peace.

Exodus 20:13 (KJV)
13 Thou shalt not kill.

Dr. Lydia A. Woods

Puzzling

Genesis 1:26 (KJV)

Genesis 1:26 (KJV)
26 And God said, Let us make man in our image, after our likeness: and let them have dominion over the fish of the sea, and over the fowl of the air, and over the cattle, and over all the earth, and over every creeping thing that creepeth upon the earth.

Sabbath Day

Exodus 20:8-11; Luke 6:5 (KJV)

Exodus 20:8-11 (KJV)
8 Remember the sabbath day, to keep it holy.
9 Six days shalt thou labour, and do all thy work:
10 But the seventh day is the sabbath of the LORD thy God: in it thou shalt not do any work, thou, nor thy son, nor thy daughter, thy manservant, nor thy maidservant, nor thy cattle, nor thy stranger that is within thy gates:
11 For in six days the LORD made heaven and earth, the sea, and all that in them is, and rested the seventh day: wherefore the LORD blessed the sabbath day, and hallowed it.

Luke 6:5 (KJV)
5 And he said unto them, That the Son of man is Lord also of the sabbath.

Dr. Lydia A. Woods

Seeds of Self-Destruction

James 1:26, 3:5-10; Proverbs 18:21, 25:23 (KJV)

James 1:26 (KJV)
26 If any man among you seem to be religious, and bridleth not his tongue, but deceiveth his own heart, this man's religion is vain.

James 3:5-10 (KJV)
5 Even so the tongue is a little member, and boasteth great things. Behold, how great a matter a little fire kindleth!
6 And the tongue is a fire, a world of iniquity: so is the tongue among our members, that it defileth the whole body, and setteth on fire the course of nature; and it is set on fire of hell.
7 For every kind of beasts, and of birds, and of serpents, and of things in the sea, is tamed, and hath been tamed of mankind:
8 But the tongue can no man tame; it is an unruly evil, full of deadly poison.
9 Therewith bless we God, even the Father; and therewith curse we men, which are made after the similitude of God.
10 Out of the same mouth proceedeth blessing and cursing. My brethren, these things ought not so to be.

Proverbs 18:21 (KJV)
21 Death and life are in the power of the tongue: and they that love it shall eat the fruit thereof.

Proverbs 25:23 (KJV)
23 The north wind driveth away rain: so doth an angry countenance a backbiting tongue.

Take No Thought

Luke 12:22-30 (KJV)

Luke 12:22-30 (KJV)
22 And he said unto his disciples, Therefore I say unto you, Take no thought for your life, what ye shall eat; neither for the body, what ye shall put on.
23 The life is more than meat, and the body is more than raiment.
24 Consider the ravens: for they neither sow nor reap; which neither have storehouse nor barn; and God feedeth them: how much more are ye better than the fowls?
25 And which of you with taking thought can add to his stature one cubit?
26 If ye then be not able to do that thing which is least, why take ye thought for the rest?
27 Consider the lilies how they grow: they toil not, they spin not; and yet I say unto you, that Solomon in all his glory was not arrayed like one of these.
28 If then God so clothe the grass, which is to day in the field, and to morrow is cast into the oven; how much more will he clothe you, O ye of little faith?
29 And seek not ye what ye shall eat, or what ye shall drink, neither be ye of doubtful mind.
30 For all these things do the nations of the world seek after: and your Father knoweth that ye have need of these things.

Dr. Lydia A. Woods

There But For the Grace...

Luke 10:27-37; Matthew 22:39 (KJV)

Luke 10:27-37 (KJV)

27 And he answering said, Thou shalt love the Lord thy God with all thy heart, and with all thy soul, and with all thy strength, and with all thy mind; and thy neighbour as thyself.
28 And he said unto him, Thou hast answered right: this do, and thou shalt live.
29 But he, willing to justify himself, said unto Jesus, And who is my neighbour?
30 And Jesus answering said, A certain man went down from Jerusalem to Jericho, and fell among thieves, which stripped him of his raiment, and wounded him, and departed, leaving him half dead.
31 And by chance there came down a certain priest that way: and when he saw him, he passed by on the other side.
32 And likewise a Levite, when he was at the place, came and looked on him, and passed by on the other side.
33 But a certain Samaritan, as he journeyed, came where he was: and when he saw him, he had compassion on him,
34 And went to him, and bound up his wounds, pouring in oil and wine, and set him on his own beast, and brought him to an inn, and took care of him.
35 And on the morrow when he departed, he took out two pence, and gave them to the host, and said unto him, Take care of him; and whatsoever thou spendest more, when I come again, I will repay thee.
36 Which now of these three, thinkest thou, was neighbour unto him that fell among the thieves?
37 And he said, He that shewed mercy on him. Then said Jesus unto him, Go, and do thou likewise.

Acceptance with Joy

Matthew 22:39 (KJV)
³⁹ And the second is like unto it, Thou shalt love thy neighbour as thyself.

Tower of Babel

Genesis 11:1-10 (KJV)

Genesis 11:1-10 (KJV)
[1] And the whole earth was of one language, and of one speech.

[2] And it came to pass, as they journeyed from the east, that they found a plain in the land of Shinar; and they dwelt there.

[3] And they said one to another, Go to, let us make brick, and burn them thoroughly. And they had brick for stone, and slime had they for morter.

[4] And they said, Go to, let us build us a city and a tower, whose top may reach unto heaven; and let us make us a name, lest we be scattered abroad upon the face of the whole earth.

[5] And the LORD came down to see the city and the tower, which the children of men builded.

[6] And the LORD said, Behold, the people is one, and they have all one language; and this they begin to do: and now nothing will be restrained from them, which they have imagined to do.

[7] Go to, let us go down, and there confound their language, that they may not understand one another's speech.

[8] So the LORD scattered them abroad from thence upon the face of all the earth: and they left off to build the city.

[9] Therefore is the name of it called Babel; because the LORD did there confound the language of all the earth: and from thence did the LORD scatter them abroad upon the face of all the earth.

[10] These are the generations of Shem: Shem was an hundred years old, and begat Arphaxad two years after the flood:

True Way of Life

John 13:34-35, 14:6 (KJV)

John 13:34-35 (KJV)
34 A new commandment I give unto you, That ye love one another; as I have loved you, that ye also love one another.
35 By this shall all men know that ye are my disciples, if ye have love one to another.

John 14:6 (KJV)
6 Jesus saith unto him, I am the way, the truth, and the life: no man cometh unto the Father, but by me.

Dr. Lydia A. Woods

What's Your Problem?

Mark 16:15-18 (KJV)

Mark 16:15-18 (KJV)
15 And he said unto them, Go ye into all the world, and preach the gospel to every creature.
16 He that believeth and is baptized shall be saved; but he that believeth not shall be damned.
17 And these signs shall follow them that believe; In my name shall they cast out devils; they shall speak with new tongues;
18 They shall take up serpents; and if they drink any deadly thing, it shall not hurt them; they shall lay hands on the sick, and they shall recover.

Scriptural Index

Genesis

1:3
   He's Good At..., 205, 380
1:9
   He's Good At..., 205, 380
1:12
   He's Good At..., 205, 380
1:16
   He's Good At..., 205, 380
1:24
   He's Good At..., 205, 380
1:26
   Puzzling, 221, 393
1:26-27
   The Day of His Birth, 7, 249
1:27
   He's Good At..., 205, 380
1:31
   He's Good At..., 205, 380
2:8-9
   My God Isn't Stupid!, 175, 359
3:1-24
   Doin' the Adam, 109, 322
3:15
   What's His Face?, 43, 276
3:22-24
   Bringing His Family Out, 5, 247
11:1-10
   Tower of Babel, 229, 399
12:2
   Just a Family Feud, 211, 384
12:3
   I'm Not Lucky – I'm Blessed!, 121, 329
17:6
   Just a Family Feud, 211, 384
18:18
   Just a Family Feud, 211, 384
22:1-19
   God Will Provide, 63, 290

24:1-67
   How Will I Know Him?, 72, 297
26:4
   I'm Not Lucky – I'm Blessed!, 121, 329
27:1-46
   Birthright, 3, 240
28:1-22
   Birthright, 3, 240
37:2-5
   Joseph, 25, 264
37:9
   Joseph, 25, 264
37:15
   Joseph, 25, 264
37:31-35
   Joseph, 25, 264
41:41-43
   Joseph, 25, 264
45:1-5
   Joseph, 25, 264

Exodus

11:2
   Doin' the Israelite, 9, 250
12:12-14
   Get in the House, 117, 327
13:21
   Doin' the Israelite, 9, 250
14:27-28
   Doin' the Israelite, 9, 250
16:2-3
   Doin' the Israelite, 9, 250
16:12
   Doin' the Israelite, 9, 250
17:2-4
   Doin' the Israelite, 9, 250
20:8-11
   Sabbath Day, 223
20:13
   Pro-Choice?, 392

Acceptance with Joy

Pro-Choice?, 219
20:8-11
   Sabbath Day, 394
Deuteronomy
7:3-14
   I'm Not Lucky – I'm Blessed!, 121, 329
Job
2:13
   So Be Like Job, 41, 275
9:10
   Has Done, Is Doing or Will Do, 161, 354
Psalms
25:3
   Just Wait!, 130, 334
27:14
   Just Wait!, 130, 334
31:19
   Simply Because You Are Mine, 39, 274
35:28
   Has Done, Is Doing or Will Do, 161, 354
37:18
   Just Wait!, 130, 334
40:5
   Has Done, Is Doing or Will Do, 161, 354
46:10
   Be Still, 105, 320
71:15
   Has Done, Is Doing or Will Do, 161, 354
91:1-16
   Hedge of Protection, 67, 294
91:11
   Children of the King, 107, 321
105:15
   The U.P.S. Man, 187, 366

111:10
   The Gift, 159, 353
118:6
   Fear vs Faith, 57, 283
119:105
   I Need the Eyes of Jesus, 73, 304
127:3-5
   A Blessing – Not a Curse!, 195, 372
   Generations in You, 158, 352
128:3
   Generations in You, 158, 352
Proverbs
1:7
   Father Knows Best, 111, 325
   Getting to Know You, 15, 253
2:1
   Getting to Know You, 15, 253
3:1-4
   Getting to Know You, 15, 253
3:5-6
   Common Sense, 199, 375
   Lean Not, 133, 337
16:16-25
   The Gift, 159, 353
18:21
   Seeds of Self-Destruction, 225, 395
19:21
   If You Want to Make God Laugh!, 75, 305
22:6
   Adult vs Child, 47, 278
25:23
   Seeds of Self-Destruction, 225, 395
Isaiah
14:27
   He's Good At..., 205, 380

40:31
   Just Wait!, 130, 334
46:9-11
   He's Good At..., 205, 381
   If You Want to Make God
     Laugh!, 75, 305
54:13
   Boys Into Men, 149, 347
64:4
   Simply Because You Are Mine,
     39, 274

Hosea
2:19
   With His Own Blood, 189, 369

Malachi
3:10
   Unable to Receive, 139, 341
3:13-17
   So What's-Up With That!, 135, 339
3:13-18
   Don't Envy Those, 53, 281
   Quest for Salvation, 37, 273

Matthew
4:1
   Master of Masters, 31, 268
4:1-11
   Know Your Enemy, 131, 335
   No Abundance in the
     Wilderness, 33, 271
4:6
   Children of the King, 107, 321
   If Thou Be..., 207, 382
4:19
   Master of Masters, 31, 268
4:23
   The Kingdom is Like Unto..., 213, 385
5:1
   Master of Masters, 31, 268

5:10-12
   With Persecution..., 141, 342
5:36
   If You Want to Make God
     Laugh!, 75, 305
6:25-34
   It's Not About Money, 83, 309
7:11
   Simply Because You Are Mine,
     39, 274
7:29
   Master of Masters, 31, 268
8:12
   Group Three, 65, 292
8:26
   Master of Masters, 31, 268
11:5
   Master of Masters, 31, 268
13:10-11
   The Kingdom is Like Unto..., 213, 385
13:31-33
   The Kingdom is Like Unto..., 213, 385
13:37-43
   Group Three, 65, 292
16:18
   The Building You Call Church, 151, 348
18:3
   Adult vs Child, 47, 278
18:20
   Don't Forsake the Assembly, 152, 349
20:1-16
   The Kingdom is Like Unto..., 213, 385
20:26
   If You Will Be Great, 209, 383

21:24
  A Bible Character, 1, 237
22:39
  There But For the Grace..., 228, 397
23:25
  The Inside of the Cup, 81, 307
24:14
  The Kingdom is Like Unto..., 213, 387
24:21-22
  Bringing His Family Out, 5, 247
25:1-30
  The Kingdom is Like Unto..., 213, 387

Mark
1:14-15
  Bringing His Family Out, 5, 247
3:4
  Pro-Choice?, 392
  Pro-Choice?, 219
3:24-25
  Denominations, 203, 377
11:25-26
  Forgive or Forgive Not, 204, 379
13:20
  For the Elect's Sake, 113, 326
  The Time is Short!, 97, 314
13:24-27
  Good News, 17, 254
15:1
  A Bible Character, 1, 237
15:10-11
  A Bible Character, 1, 237
16:1
  A Bible Character, 1, 237
16:15-18
  Good News II, 19, 256

What's Your Problem?, 233, 401
16:15-20
  Just Do It!, 29, 267
16:17
  Know Your Enemy, 131, 336

Luke
2:6-14
  The Day of His Birth, 7, 249
2:7
  God's M.O., 119, 328
2:26
  Somethin' Told Me, 91, 311
4:18
  I Need the Eyes of Jesus, 73, 304
4:18-19
  Get a Testimony, 13, 252
6:34-38
  Just Give It!, 169, 357
6:37
  Forgive or Forgive Not, 204, 379
6:38
  Unable to Receive, 139, 341
8:43-48
  Master of Masters, 31, 268
10:27-37
  There But For the Grace..., 228, 397
11:39
  The Inside of the Cup, 81, 307
12:22-30
  Take No Thought, 227, 396
12:22-34
  It's Not About Money, 83, 308
12:32
  Fear vs Faith, 57, 283
13:24-30
  Group Three, 65, 292

18:16
   Adult vs Child, 47, 278
22:47
   A Bible Character, 1, 237
22:57
   A Bible Character, 1, 237
22:60
   A Bible Character, 1, 237
23:21-34
   A Bible Character, 1, 237

John
1:1-5
   Ain't He All That!, 193, 371
1:12-13
   Holy Rollers, 163, 355
2:1-11
   Master of Masters, 31, 268
3:1
   Children of the King, 107, 321
3:9
   Children of the King, 107, 321
4:44
   The U.P.S. Man, 187, 366
8:12
   Oh! To be Like the Master, 85, 310
8:28-29
   Oh! To be Like the Master, 85, 310
8:31
   Oh! To be Like the Master, 85, 310
11:43-44
   Master of Masters, 31, 268
12:26
   Somethin' Told Me, 91, 311
13:34-35
   True Way of Life, 231, 400
   Was He Saved? Did He Know the Lord?, 99, 317

14:1-4
   E.T., 153, 350
14:6
   True Way of Life, 231, 400
14:13
   Above All, 103, 319
16:33
   Answer to Many a Prayer, 145, 345
   I'm Tired!, 123, 331
19:11
   What's His Face?, 43, 276

Acts
1:3-4
   Take a Visit to the Upper Room, 93, 312
1:7
   The Time is Short!, 97, 314
1:8
   Take a Visit to the Upper Room, 93, 312
2:1-21
   Take a Visit to the Upper Room, 93, 312
2:17
   Bringing His Family Out, 5, 247
20:28
   Blood Disguise, 147, 346
   With His Own Blood, 189, 369
20:35
   Just Give It!, 169, 357

Romans
1:21-32
   Upside Down, Inside Out, 188, 367
1:26-27
   Love You - Not Your Sin, 215, 390

5:3
   Answer to Many a Prayer, 145, 345
5:19
   Obedience the Highest Form of Praise, 177, 361
6:3-4
   Liar, Liar, 171, 358
7:14-21
   The Perfect Murder, 179, 362
7:14-25
   Convicted, 201, 376
8:15
   Fear vs Faith, 57, 283
8:16
   Take Out the Trash!, 137, 340
8:26
   If You Loved Me Lord…, 127, 332
12:12
   Answer to Many a Prayer, 145, 345

I Corinthians
1:9
   Cerebral Palsy, 198, 374
1:25
   Common Sense, 199, 375
1:26-27
   God's M.O., 119, 328
2:7
   God's M.O., 119, 328
2:9-11
   Simply Because You Are Mine, 39, 274
2:12
   Bringing His Family Out, 5, 247
3:7-9
   The Family Business, 55, 282

3:16
   I Need the Eyes of Jesus, 73, 304
3:19
   Common Sense, 199, 375
   God's M.O., 119, 328
6:17
   Resistance is Futile, 181, 363
12:12-27
   Resistance is Futile, 181, 363
12:12-31
   Denominations, 203, 377
15:3
   Good News, 17, 254
15:52
   Good News, 17, 254

II Corinthians
4:9-18
   With Persecution…, 141, 342
5:7
   Common Sense, 199, 375
6:16
   Only Human!, 391
5:17
   Only Human!, 391
   Only Human!, 217
6:16
   Not in a Place Called Church, 176, 360
   Only Human!, 217
10:5
   In a Split Second, 77, 306

Galatians
4:5-7
   It's Adoption Time, 21, 262
4:6
   Created in My Father's Image, 51, 280
5:22-23
   Fruit Trees, 155, 351

Ephesians
1:3-6
  Bringing His Family Out, 5, 247
1:4-5
  It's Adoption Time, 21, 262
1:7
  Blood Disguise, 147, 346
3:5
  God's M.O., 119, 328
3:10
  Above All, 103, 319
4:30
  Somethin' Told Me, 91, 311
5:3-5
  I'm Tired!, 123, 331
5:27
  The Building You Call Church, 151, 348
6:10-17
  It's War!, 23, 263
6:11-17
  Put It All On!, 35, 272
6:18
  But For Your Praying Saints, 49, 279
  Take Out the Trash!, 137, 340

Philippians
1:6
  Cerebral Palsy, 198, 374
2:6
  Created in My Father's Image, 51, 280
2:8
  Obedience the Highest Form of Praise, 177, 361
4:19
  How Many Times, 69, 296
  Love is an Action, 134, 338

Colossians
1:18
  The Building You Call Church, 151, 348

I Thessalonians
5:1-2
  The Time is Short!, 97, 314
5:17
  But For Your Praying Saints, 49, 279
  Take Out the Trash!, 137, 340
5:24
  Cerebral Palsy, 198, 374

II Timothy
2:11
  Liar, Liar, 171, 358
2:15
  Not in a Place Called Church, 176, 360

Hebrews
1:2-3
  Ain't He All That!, 193, 371
5:8
  Jesus Learned Obedience, 165, 356
  Obedience the Highest Form of Praise, 177, 361
9:22
  Blood Disguise, 147, 346
10:25
  Don't Forsake the Assembly, 152, 349
10:38
  Bringing His Family Out, 5, 247
12:1
  So Great a Cloud of Witnesses, 183, 365
12:6
  Boys Into Men, 149, 347

James
1:2-4
　Get a Testimony, 13, 252
1:5
　Father Knows Best, 111, 325
　It's Alright, 129, 333
　Lean Not, 133, 337
1:8
　In a Split Second, 77, 306
1:26
　Seeds of Self-Destruction, 225, 395
2:12
　Get in the House, 117, 327
2:18-19
　Get in the House, 117, 327
3:5-10
　Seeds of Self-Destruction, 225, 395
4:3
　If You Loved Me Lord…, 127, 332
5:13
　Take Out the Trash!, 137, 340
5:16
　But For Your Praying Saints, 49, 279

I Peter
1:23
　Holy Rollers, 163, 355
2:9
　A Bible Character, 1, 237
　Bringing His Family Out, 5, 247
　Call My Name, 197, 373
　Holy Rollers, 163, 355
3:4-6
　Hedge of Protection, 67, 295
5:3
　If You Will Be Great, 209, 383

II Peter
2:1-3
　Not in a Place Called Church, 176, 360
3
　The Time is Short!, 97, 314

I John
4:18
　Fear vs Faith, 57, 283
4:21
　Was He Saved? Did He Know the Lord?, 99, 317
5:1
　Holy Rollers, 163, 355
5:14
　Above All, 103, 319

Revelations
1:7
　Good News, 17, 254
2:1-29
　Go the Distance, 59, 284
　Good News II, 19, 256
3:1-22
　Go the Distance, 59, 286
　Good News II, 19, 256
3:19
　Boys Into Men, 149, 347
19:7-9
　Good News, 17, 254
　With His Own Blood, 189, 369
20:1-3
　Good News, 17, 254
21:1-5
　Good News, 17, 254
21:9
　With His Own Blood, 189, 369
22:13
　Ain't He All That!, 193, 371

Alphabetical Listing of Poems

Dr. Lydia A. Woods

Above All, 103
Adult vs Child, 47
Ain't He All That!, 193
Answer to Many a Prayer, 145
Be Still!, 105
A Bible Character, 1
Birthright, 3
A Blessing – Not a Curse!, 195
Blood Disguise, 147
Boys Into Men, 149
Bringing His Family Out 5
The Building You Call Church, 151
But For Your Praying Saints, 49
Call My Name, 197
Cerebral Palsy, 198
Children of the King, 107
Common Sense, 199
Convicted, 201
Created in My Father's Image, 51
The Day of His Birth, 7
Denominations, 203
Doin' the Israelite, 9
Doin' the Adam, 109
Don't Forsake the Assembly, 152
Don't Envy Those, 53
E.T., 153
The Family Business, 55
Father Knows Best, 111
Fear vs Faith, 57
For the Elect's Sake, 113
Forgive or Forgive Not, 204
Fruit Trees, 155
Generations in You, 158
Get a Testimony, 13
Get in the House, 117
Getting to Know You, 15
The Gift, 159
Go the Distance, 59
God Will Provide, 63
God's M.O., 119

Good News, 17
Good News II, 19
Group Three, 65
Has Done, Is Doing or Will Do, 161
He's Good At…, 205
Hedge of Protection, 67
Holy Rollers, 163
How Many Times, 69
How Will I Know Him?, 72
I Need the Eyes of Jesus, 73
I'm Not Lucky – I'm Blessed!, 121
I'm Tired!, 123
If Thou Be…, 207
If You Loved Me Lord…, 127
If You Want to Make God Laugh!, 75
If You Will Be Great. 209
In a Split Second, 77
The Inside of the Cup, 81
It's Adoption Time, 21
It's Alright, 129
It's Not About Money, 83
It's War!, 23
Jesus Learned Obedience, 165
Joseph, 25
Just a Family Feud, 211
Just Do It!, 29
Just Give It!, 169
Just Wait!, 130
The Kingdom is Like Unto…, 213
Know Your Enemy, 131
Lean Not, 133
Liar, Liar, 171
Love is an Action, 134
Love You - Not Your Sin, 215
Master of Masters, 31
My God Isn't Stupid!, 175
No Abundance in the Wilderness, 33
Not in a Place Called Church, 176

-413-

A Compilation of Christian Poetry   *Alphabetical Listing of Poems*

Obedience the Highest Form of Praise, 177
Oh! To be Like the Master, 85
Only Human!, 217
The Perfect Murder, 179
Pro-Choice?, 219
Put It All On!, 35
Puzzling, 221
Quest for Salvation, 37
Resistance is Futile, 181
Sabbath Day, 223
Seeds of Self-Destruction, 225
Simply Because You Are Mine, 39
So Be Like Job, 41
So Great a Cloud of Witnesses, 183
So What's-Up With That!, 135
Somethin' Told Me, 91
Take a Visit to the Upper Room, 93
Take No Thought, 227
Take Out the Trash!, 137
There But For the Grace..., 228
The Time is Short!, 97
Tower of Babel, 229
True Way of Life, 231
Unable to Receive, 139
The U.P.S. Man, 187
Upside Down, Inside Out, 188
Was He Saved? Did He Know the Lord?, 99
What's His Face?, 43
What's Your Problem?, 233
With His Own Blood, 189
With Persecution..., 141

www.ingramcontent.com/pod-product-compliance
Lightning Source LLC
Chambersburg PA
CBHW071234160426
43196CB00009B/1051